Fingers Pointing
Towards the Moon

Also by Wei Wu Wei

WHY LAZARUS LAUGHED

ASK THE AWAKENED

ALL ELSE IS BONDAGE

OPEN SECRET

THE TENTH MAN

POSTHUMOUS PIECES

UNWORLDLY WISE

Fingers Pointing Towards the Moon

Reflections of a Pilgrim on the Way

WEI WU WEI

SENTIENT PUBLICATIONS, LLC

First Sentient Publications edition, 2003

Copyright © 2003 by Kegan Paul Limited.
Reprinted in the United States by Sentient Publications, by
arrangement with Kegan Paul Limited, London.

Printed in the United States of America

Grateful acknowledgment is made for permission to use
Matt Errey's editorial notes.

Cover design by Kim Johansen, Black Dog Design
Book design by Anna Bergstrom

Library of Congress Cataloging-in-Publication Data

Wei, Wu Wei
   Fingers pointing towards the moon : reflections of a pilgrim
on the way / Wei Wu Wei.—1st Sentient Publications ed.
      p. cm.
   Includes index.
   ISBN 1-59181-010-8
   1. Religious life—Zen Buddhism. 2. Zen Buddhism—
Doctrines. 3. Religious life—Taoism. 4. Taoism—Doctrines.
I. Title.
BQ9286 .W45 2003
294.3'44--dc22
                                        2003014066

SENTIENT PUBLICATIONS
A Limited Liability Company
1113 Spruce St.
Boulder, CO 80302
www.sentientpublications.com

Contents

Foreword   vii

Preface   xi

1. Reality and Manifestation I   1
2. Time and Space I   4
3. Reality and Manifestation II   12
4. Time and Space II   15
5. Work and Play I   15
6. Reality and Manifestation III   17
7. Time and Space III   18
8. Physics and Metaphysics I   21
9. Work and Play II   22
10. Physics and Metaphysics II   23
11. Time and Space IV   28
12. Physics and Metaphysics III   31
13. Reality and Manifestation IV   32
14. Work and Play III   41
15. Reality and Manifestation V   44
16. Physics and Metaphysics IV   48
17. Time and Space V   50
18. Reality and Manifestation VI   51
19. Time and Space VI   63
20. Work and Play IV   65
21. Reality and Manifestation VII   67
22. The Ego I   67
23. Physics and Metaphysics V   71
24. Reality and Manifestation VIII   76
25. Physics and Metaphysics VI   79
26. Time and Space VII   81
27. Physics and Metaphysics VII   82
28. Reality and Manifestation IX   85

29. Physics and Metaphysics VIII   87
30. Reality and Manifestation X   93
31. Work and Play V   97
32. Time and Space VIII   98
33. Reality and Manifestation XI   99
34. Time and Space IX   100
35. The Ego II   101
36. Brief Causeries I   102
37. Brief Causeries II   103
38. Brief Causeries III   105
39. Brief Causeries IV   106
40. Physics and Metaphysics IX   108
41. Brief Causeries V   111
42. Work and Play VI   113
43. Reality and Manifestation XII   115
44. Work and Play VII   117
45. Reality and Manifestation XIII   118
46. Work and Play VIII   120
47. Physics and Metaphysics X   121
48. Reality and Manifestation XIV   124
49. Physics and Metaphysics XI   126
50. Work and Play IX   129
51. Time and Space X   137
52. Work and Play X   139
53. Time and Space XI   140
54. Work and Play XI   145
55. Reality and Manifestation XV   146
56. Time and Space XII   148
57. Work and Play XII   149
58. Reality and Manifestation XVI   150
59. Time and Space XIII   152
60. Vale   153

Colophon   155

Index   157

Foreword

Wei Wu Wei says:

The implied Unicity, the totality of undivided mind, is itself a concept of its own division or duality, for relatively—relativity being relative to what itself is—it cannot be conceived or known at all.

All that could ever be known about it is simply that, being Absolute, it must necessarily be devoid of any kind of objective existence whatever, other than that of the totality of all possible phenomena which constitute its relative appearance.

What does Wei Wu Wei mean by this statement? I think what he means is precisely what I mean when I say:

Consciousness is all there is; other than Consciousness, nothing is. And this is a concept.

I have been giving talks at my residence in Bombay every morning for the last several years. I always keep repeating:

Make no mistake: whatever I say—whatever its impact—is a concept. It is not the truth. A concept is something that someone may accept and someone may not. The Truth is that which no one can deny. And therefore the only Truth, in phenomenality, is "I AM"—the impersonal Awareness of Being.

On this basis, whatever any sage has ever said, whatever any scripture of any religion says is a concept.

When I wrote the preface for my first book, *Pointers from Nisargadatta Maharaj*, I had included the following paragraph in it:

> As I was translating Shri Maharaj's talks into English, I began noticing in my translations the distinct influence of Wei Wu Wei's use of the English language in his books. I have no doubt that traces of this influence would be clearly noticed by the discerning reader in those articles. Apart from the language, it seemed to me a wondrous demonstration of the universality of the subject itself that the writings of a scholar and practitioner of the Tao philosophy like Wei Wu Wei, thousands of miles away (and hardly a popular writer), would find corroboration in the words of a Self-realized Jnani like Shri Nisargadatta Maharaj, whose education, as he says himself, takes him just beyond the limit of illiteracy!

Against my better judgment, under pressure from several well-wishers, this paragraph was dropped: the argument was that what I was in effect doing was to place a mere writer on the same level with Maharaj, a Self-realized Jnani.

The whole story is that Wei Wu Wei's book, *Open Secret*, was given to me as a gift by a friend of mine more than a decade before I started going to Maharaj. When I first read it, I could not make any sense out of it, except that I had the good fortune to realize that this book was a real treasure; and I kept it aside so that it would not get thrown out with other books during one of the routine clean-ups. And then, for some unfathomable reason, the thought suddenly occurred to me about the book almost immediately after I started visiting Maharaj. I cannot describe the innumerable intellectual frustrations I went through between the two of them—Nisargadatta Maharaj and Wei Wu Wei. I repeatedly felt that the two of them had ganged up to have a private joke of their own at my expense. It was indeed a gang-up but, as I realized some time later, it was to bring about a sudden awakening in this body-mind mechanism called Ramesh.

When I started reading Wei Wu Wei, I used to marvel at the command of the English language that a Chinese man should have acquired. It was some time later that I gathered that Wei Wu Wei was not a Chinese but a wealthy Irish aristocrat (Terrence Gray), highly educated at Oxford University, an authority on wines and race horses!

I got this information through a lady who used to visit Maharaj. She later sent me a photograph of Wei Wu Wei with her. He was a giant of a man. She mentioned *Pointers from Nisargadatta Maharaj* to him and he expressed a desire to see the book. I sent a copy of the book to him at his villa in the South of France, with a letter expressing my gratitude for the guidance I had received from his books. Unfortunately at that time (W. W.W. was almost 90 years of age) senility was beginning to set in; and his wife had to read out the book (*Pointers*) to him in his lucid moments. W.W.W. indicated that he enjoyed the book. Our mutual friend told me that he referred to *Pointers* as "Wei Wu Wei without tears." I could at once relate the reference to the play on the London stage—in the late thirties when I was a student in London—named *French Without Tears.* W.W.W. died in 1986 at the age of 91.

I gathered that his principal mentor was Ramana Maharshi, of Tiruvannamalai, who has been my earliest inspiration since I was twelve years old. The core of W.W.W.'s understanding is non-doership. As the Buddha has put it: "Events happen, deeds are done, but there is no individual doer thereof."

It is interesting that the Hindu scripture says, "Thou art the doer, Thou art the experiencer; Thou art the speaker and Thou art the listener." This obviously means: you may think you are the speaker and the "other" is the listener, and vice versa; but the truth is that it is the Primal Energy functioning through two human body-mind instruments producing the speaking through one instrument and the listening through the other.

RAMESH S. BALSEKAR
Bombay, India
26 February 2003

Preface

I wonder why this collection of observations and suggestions is not signed with the personal name of an "author," as books usually are?

Is the person responsible modest? Is he ashamed of them? Perhaps he does not wish those who would not understand to associate him with ideas of this kind? Is it pride? Is it humility?

What is a name? (Is it not the symbol of someone who regards himself as a separate individual?) Is not a name essentially—the name of an ego? But the Self, the Principal, the I-Reality has no name. ("The Tao that can be named is not the real Tao": one of the greatest books in the world opens with those words.)

May we see in this the pretension that these thoughts are of someone who lives on the plane of Reality? But were that so would not the Fingers have been pointing AT the moon?

No doubt the fact itself is of little interest, but its implications may be worth this consideration. Perhaps the explanation is simpler than any of these suppositions.

Tom, Dick, and Harry think they have written the books that they sign (or painted the pictures, composed the music, built the churches). But they exaggerate. It was a pen that did it, or some other implement. They held the pen? Yes, but the hand that held the pen was an implement too, and the brain that controlled the hand. They were intermediaries, instruments, just apparatus. Even the best apparatus does not need a personal name like Tom, Dick, or Harry.

If the nameless builders of the Taj Mahal, of Chartres, of Rheims, of a hundred cathedral symphonies, knew that—and avoided the solecism of attributing to their own egos the works that were created through their instrumentality—may not even a jotter-down of passing metaphysical notions know it also?

If you should not understand this—give the book away before reading it! But give it to a pilgrim on the Way. Why? Because it would have helped the pilgrim who compiled it, if it had been given to him, and that is why he compiled it, and why he presumes to offer it to other pilgrims.

But in case you should still wonder who is responsible for this book I do not know how to do better than to inscribe the words

WEI WU WEI

1 ·~ Reality and Manifestation - I

Aspects of Not-Being, 1

It is less what one is that should matter, than what one is not.

To acquire knowledge should not be our first aim, but rather to rid ourselves of ignorance—which is false-knowledge.

The qualities we possess should never be a matter for satisfaction, but the qualities we have discarded.

If Charity (compassion), Simplicity, and Humility are desirable as attributes that is because they depend upon the elimination of qualities that have been discarded.

Behind the Conditioned is the Unconditioned. Behind Being is Not-Being. Behind Action is Non-Action (not inaction). Behind Me is Not-Me. "I am Not-I, therefore I am I": the Prajnaparamita Sutra said it a thousand years ago. Transform "I" into "Not-I" and then "Not-I" will become "I." Only God is "I" (I am only "I" in so far as I am God or the Absolute, i.e. my Principle).

Does not one of our elementary errors lie in imagining that we "do" things, for it seems to be equally probable that things "do" us? We believe that we perform an endless series of actions, but the truth may be that an endless series of actions performs us. We think that we manipulate events, but are we not rather manipulated by events? We think we go to meet that which we experience, but that which we experience may come to meet us. It is perhaps an illusion that we "live": we are "lived."

"Take Life as it comes," we say—that is be aware that it is life that comes to us and not we who go to life.

What we call "life" is only things that happen. The patent (acquired) personality reacts to "life" with states of mind. The latent personality should be unaffected by 'life': it need not "do" and is content to "be."

The Buddha-nature is the unconditioned nature.

It is not for us to search but to remain still, to achieve Immobility not Action.

We only exist in the instant: we do not exist as a continuity, as we suppose. Our apparent existence from day to day, year to year, is an illusion; but we exist in each instant *between* the ticking of the clock of Time, each instant not one of which are we quick enough to perceive.

Action and Non-Action, 1

Non-Action on the plane of Being becomes, by articulation, Correct-Action on the plane of Existing.

Correct-Action may be anything from violence to what we regard as inaction—for inaction is inevitably a form of action.

The majority of our actions are Incorrect-Action. We are mad monkeys eternally doing unnecessary things, obsessed with the necessity of "doing," terrified of inaction, glorifying "doers" almost uncritically, regardless of the havoc they cause, scorning "non-doers," equally uncritically, blind to the prosperity that follows in their wake, the former being the normal result of what is Incorrect-Action, the latter being the normal result of inaction that is Correct-Action.

But what we regard as action is really reaction, the reaction of our artificial and impermanent ego to the non-ego, to external events. We react from morning to night: we do not act.

That, I think, is the explanation of the Taoist doctrine of Non-Action. Explanation is necessary because translation from the Chinese ideograms does not reveal the difference between Non-Action that is noumenal and inaction that is phenomenal.

The dynamism of inaction in a given circumstance can be greater than that of action in the same circumstance. Inaction that is dynamic requires vision and self-control—for action is easier to us than inaction. It is the dynamism of inaction that identifies it as Correct-Action.

We are brought up to believe that in all circumstances we should "do." Rather than face inaction we spend hours drinking spirits or consuming narcotics. Therein we are reagents only: we "do" but we know not how to BE.

Correct-Action should be normal to the man who has realised his state of Satori, for his ego, dissolved or integrated, is no longer in a position to react. In consequence all his actions should be Correct-Action.

But Correct-Action must be possible to us also in both its forms. Action based on affectivity, positive or negative, action based on reasoning, dependent upon the comparison of the opposites, and thereby relative, involving memory, manifestations of the illusory ego, is unlikely to be correct—for they are not action but reaction.

It would seem, therefore, that Correct-Action can only be spontaneous—the product of the split-second that outwits the fraud of Time.

Note: The term "Correct-Action" is an approximation only, as would be the French "l'Action Juste." Two additional terms could follow it in brackets in order to develop its meaning more fully. These words are "necessary" and "real." One may read, therefore, each time, "Correct, Necessary, Real Action," and "Incorrect, Unnecessary, Unreal Action." But the more technical term "Adequate (and Inadequate) Action," when understood, is still better.

❧

The dynamic inaction referred to above is a form of Adequate-Action which on the plane of Being is Non-Action. But negative inaction, which is a mode of our habitual action, and which is reaction, partakes of the unreality of that. Both action and inaction, in our normal forms of manifestation, are on the plane of phenomena and have no real existence.

There are, therefore, two forms of Action, real and unreal, each of which has an aspect which we regard as inaction.

2 ⟶ Time and Space - I

Past and Future, 1

A phenomenon is something that occurs in three-dimensional space interpreted with the fourth dimension seen serially as time.

Reality (noumenon) is motionless, ubiquitous, and permanent.

If there were no memory there would be no Past. If there were no desire or fear there would be no Future. The Present, renewed every instant, alone would remain, and it would be eternity for there could be no Time.

In our existing condition we only know the Past and imagine the Future; the Present never exists for us—for it is always a memory before we are able to conceive it.

Have the Past and the Future any reality? We have every reason to ask. May the Past not be merely a trick of memory? May the Future not be only a fabrication for the fulfillment of desire? Can there be anything but an eternal Present?

Our concept of Time, but not our percept, as of something in flux, is probably mistaken. Besides, if we were in it we could not be aware that it was flowing; at least the "I" that perceives would have to be on the bank of the river, and would therefore be intemporal (outside time). It is much more probable, and others have realised it, that we ourselves are in movement and that what we observe is immobile. Like planets circling round the sun, like electrons round the nuclei of the atom, our "life" should be an orbit round reality. But our perceptions wear blinkers—they can only perceive one segment at a time, a split-second vision of a slice of reality, which we build up into a continuity, like a cinema-film made up of "stills." Unfortunately we take each slice as a thing-in-itself whereas it is merely a segment, the relative

5

reality being the totality. But the totality is not the totalisation of fragments which only represent a fraction—for we only perceive one aspect, what we know as the outside (and only one, or, at most, three sides of that) of anything whatsoever.

Differentiation

Differentiation may be a property of the Time-dimension as experienced by us.

Seen (by Observer 2 in Time 2) at right angles to the three dimensions of Space, Past and Future become Present, and (by Observer 3 in Time 3) the manifold becomes unicity.

The fourth-dimension, when seen by us serially as time (as opposed to its total aspect which is eternity) produces the illusion of phenomena. (If passing-time is illusory, i.e. is the fourth dimension of Space seen by us in a distorted form, which is serially, it is merely *seen* as one-damn-thing-after-another—for, not being able to see it at right-angles to our own dimensions we see it as a line parallel to one of them—in reality it must be at right-angles to our tridimensional world, and what seems to us to be serial is really in eternity, fixed and "permanent.")

"We create Time ourselves, as a function of our receptive apparatus," as Kant told us. Time is an imperfect sense of Space. Time is (1) Motion in (2) the Fourth Dimension.

"Time is the fourth dimension of Space," as Relativity tells us, a dimension at right-angles perceived in succession.

Motion

The dynamism we know as "Life," and consciousness thereof, are and remain four-dimensional.

Science is built on the arbitrary assumption that the universe exists in Time and Space.

There is no becoming. ALL IS.

The illusion of Motion is due to our inability to see every thing at once, to the fact that we see one thing after another. The motion is in our psyche.

Rhythms, undulations, are perhaps the curvature of Time.

Time is the measure of Motion. (Is Motion the interpretation of an angle in the fourth dimension?)

Three-dimensionality is a function of our senses. Time is the boundary of our senses.

What we know as birth and death are an effect of Time— and, as such, necessarily illusory.

The Dimensions of Space

Time is the fourth dimension perceived serially, i.e. as a succession of phenomena.
We live in the fourth dimension without perceiving it sensorially, but it is evident everywhere by inference when we know where to look for signs of it.
Duplication, the development of snow-flakes, window-frost,

the symmetry of branches of trees, growth of all kinds, radiation, electro-magnetism, motion, light, perhaps undulation, are all probably manifestations of the fourth dimension.

Our psyche exists in the fourth dimension, and our "linga sharira" (composite body which we can only see sectionally). What we see of one another are three-dimensional segments of a four-dimensional totality.

The next dimension is Eternity (in its time-aspect) and Infinity (in its space-aspect) in which everything exists immutably or is infinite variation at one point. This is the fifth dimension or the second dimension of Time, but Ouspensky states that each higher dimension is infinity for the dimension immediately below it.

The sixth dimension is that in which every possibility exists.

Eternity and Passing Time

Duration (or Eternity) is the necessary point of Immobility from which Passing-time is seen as such.

We could not be aware of Passing-time if an element of us were not situated in Duration.

Duration (Eternity seen as such) is not so much what Time becomes when it is seen at right-angles as it is the point from which Time is seen at right-angles.

Duration is the Eiffel Tower from which is seen the plane surface of the Champ de Mars with its moving figures. Seen from the top of the Eiffel Tower, from a motionless point, from one of an infinite number of motionless points, the plane surface of the Champs de Mars beneath is covered with moving objects. They move at approximately the same speed, with reference to the top of the Eiffel Tower, whether they are approaching its base or going away from it—just as light travels at approximately the same speed with reference to an observer whether the observer is moving towards or away from the source of the light (the Michelson-Morley experiment corrected by Adams). Light, therefore, would seem to be using a dimension at right-angles to those of the observer. (The fact that light is found to be two separate and incompatible things—an undulation and photons—might mean that its four-dimensional form is undulatory whereas it manifests tridimensionally as a shower of particles.)

But perhaps we should take the lift in the Eiffel Tower if we wish the light-analogy to be correct, for the speed of the lift will be unchanged with reference to observers moving towards the Eiffel Tower or away from it.

If Passing-time be represented by the two-dimensional movement of the Champ de Mars, and Duration by the Eiffel Tower itself, whatever three-dimensional (vertical) movement there may be within it (that of the lift for example), such movement, being in another dimension, and so at right-angles to all others, will be constant in reference to all movement on the plane surface of the Champ de Mars.

Revaluation of Values, 1

That part of the universe which our senses allow us to perceive is the tridimensional part, and is seen in slices.

The illusory character of Time appears to have been evident to the Greek philosophers, in particular to Heraclitus. However, such a concept proved too radical for Science and Religion, though it remained implicit in philosophy and metaphysics and became explicit once more in the words of Kant: "We create Time ourselves, as a function of our receptive apparatus." The evidence of philosophy is insufficient for Science, but in recent years Relativity has established it in the formulae "Time is the fourth dimension of Space," and "The universe is a Space-Time continuum." The ground was thereby cut from under the feet of positivist scientists, though only the great men realised it at once, or have yet realised it.

Nevertheless Time (and Space) are so fundamental to our outlook that most of our conceptions remain based upon a proven illusion.

How, for instance, can we "survive" death if death implies the disintegration of the "receptive apparatus" which fabricates Time? Any concept, survival, reincarnation, or other, that implies the notion that Time is something outside ourselves, something that goes on whether we are here or not, is evidently absurd.

Should not all our ideas be subjected immediately to this test and discarded if our notion of Time is found to be implicit in them? Is not this the initial revaluation to which all our values should be submitted?

❧

It seems clear that the invisible aspects of ourselves must lie in a further dimension, and the next higher dimension to the three that we know is the Fourth.

Reincarnation and Recurrence, 1

The only form of Reincarnation that seems to be compatible with what we are able to understand of the universe is better termed Recurrence.

It could, in fact, be supposed that our lives recur eternally, and it might be that such was the sense in which what became the popular doctrine of Reincarnation was understood and admitted by the Masters and by the Lord Buddha himself. (If the popular doctrine antedates the Masters, as is probable, then in appearing to endorse it they intended the sense of Recurrence to be understood by those few who might be capable of grasping such an esoteric concept. Evidence, real or imaginary, for this interpretation, can be found in the sutras.)

But Recurrence involves a time-factor, a repetition of the film which constitutes our life, a reliving of each one of the innumerable "stills" or slices (segments) which make up our totality (in so far as we know it), the re-experiencing of that totality serially or as one-damn-thing-after-another, and for that a receptive-apparatus (as Kant described us) with sense perceptions to recreate time would be necessary. In fact such a receptive-apparatus, i.e. every human being, having materialised tridimensionally, must exist eternally in the dimension at right-angles in every moment of its materialisation. (The intersection of Time and of Eternity being the Moment, that of the Moment and of Eternity must be Time, and that of Time and the Moment must be Eternity.)

The receptive-apparatus, therefore, exists in Eternity and so operates therein, so that the illusion of a consecutive "life" should be eternal also.

The concept of Time as a curvature—and how could it be otherwise?—makes each "life" a complete circle, self-created as an inherent characteristic of Time, and necessarily such. A circle, having neither beginning nor end, extended in two dimensions, must continue indefinitely, repeating itself as an aspect of eternity. But if it be extended in three dimensions it becomes automatically capable of infinite variations.

In both concepts, which are different aspects of the same relative truth, eternal Recurrence appears to be not merely possible but quite inevitable.

3 ⸱⸺ *Reality and Manifestation - II*

Reality and the Ego, 1

Nine-tenths of the ideas which occupy our thoughts, which are the subjects of our conversations, discussions, discourses, public and private, have no existence in Reality.

Political, ethical, and social notions are in this category. They are phantasies, make-believe, comparable with children's games of "let's pretend." (Ouspensky found that he could obtain no answer to such questions, when he was in contact with the noumenal plane, and when he sought the reason he found that it was because the questions referred to something that has no existence.)

Dogmas, religious, political, or moral, are *ipso facto* untrue. Truth itself cannot be expressed in words. Relative truth cannot be conveyed dogmatically. Yet we confound dogma with truth! (See Chap. 13: *Reality and Manifestation IV; Reality and the Ego, 2*)

The unity, and ultimate identity, of what we distinguish as Spirit and Matter, which is a metaphysical concept and a tenet of Zen, would seem to make it inevitable that what we see as "matter" may be regarded as that aspect of "spirit" which our senses are able to perceive. We perceive it as such—a fraction of it at a time—and are simple enough to suppose that what we perceive is the only reality.

We are only aware of that aspect of the universe of which

the senses we possess are able to inform us.

An insect with antennae may have only one sense: his awareness of the universe must be restricted relatively to ours. A man born blind is aware of less of the universe than a man with sight. An animal has five senses only: he has a psyche and uses it but, having percepts without concepts, is unlikely to be aware of it. A man has six senses—as oriental psychology has always understood—for he is aware of that aspect of the universe which is his mind. If we had further senses we may suppose that we should become aware of further aspects of the universe. To imagine that the universe is restricted to that of which we are aware is probably as ill-founded in our case as in that of the insect.

In the scale of colour we are only able to distinguish seven degrees, and that which is darkness to us is not darkness to the cat, while that which is darkness to birds is not so to us.

In the scale of smell many animals have a wider range than we have.

In the scales of touch and sound the blind bat has a greater sensibility than ours, as is the case with sundry insects.

Our senses have a more limited range than those of many other creatures, and a wider range than that of some. To that degree the extent of our knowledge of the universe is less, or greater, than theirs. To that degree we have experimental evidence that the universe is less, or more, restricted than the one we know.

"Birth" looks as though it were a materialisation into tridimensionality of energy from dimensions beyond the perceptive capacity of our senses. So regarded, "birth" becomes an arbitrary point in a process of growth.

When this process reaches a certain stage of development the energising factor appears to be withdrawn, which results in the dissolution of the tridimensional materialisation into the chemical constituents out of which it was constructed. This incident is known as "death."

But we are only aware of the tridimensional aspect of this phenomenon, known as "life," presented to us by our senses serially in Time. The tridimensional segments, which are all we can see of our four-dimensional totality (which is composed of everything the "living" being has been since "birth" plus everything he will be until "death"), should exist simultaneously and compose an "entity." Moreover in the further dimension at right-angles each moment of that "life," being an intersection of Time and of Eternity, eternally exists. There can, therefore, be no end to "life," every moment of which should exist simultaneously and forever.

If further senses enabled us to become aware of further aspects of the universe we might expect to perceive individuals, of every genus, associated in a manner reminiscent of the leaves of a tree—all "growing" on one branch, all attached to one trunk, all nourished by the same roots. That, perhaps, is why cats are cats, all and always cats, and why all men have approximately identical perceptions of everything they are able to know of the universe.

All awareness is subjective. Similarity in the perceptions of individuals within a genus may be due to basic *identity*.

The objective reality of the universe, if such can be supposed to exist, must forever be unknowable to Man as to Microbe.

❧

It is man's sixth sense, his awareness of his own mind, and that alone, which differentiates him from the animals, and gives him the technical superiority which he claims.

4 ·~ Time and Space - II

The Illusory Element of the Ego

Might one not say: the concept that the self-as-an-entity-distinct-from-other-entities is illusory is probably itself a false concept, for it assumes that the self has spatial characteristics?

The illusory character of the self, so much insisted upon, may well be an error due to a misplacement of the illusory element, which really belongs not to the self but to a non-existent spatial character gratuitously attributed to it.

If Space and Time are themselves illusory—as the same metaphysical approach insists—why should the self be given a spatial attribute? What is there in our consciousness of self to justify a spatial limitation?

But if the self is not in Space, as it may not be in Time, it need not be illusory. *It is then only illusory in so far as it is conceived as a spatial and temporal entity.*

Distinctness being a spatial and temporal factor, and an illusion, the false self or I-process, stripped of its temporal and spatial appearance, i.e. of its illusory element, would seem to be a manifestation of the I-Reality Itself.

5 ·~ Work and Play - I

Words, Words

Anything worth saying, it should be possible to say in a few dozen words. He who speaks diffusely understands dimly; he who understands clearly speaks concisely.

Facts and ideas ultimately are simple. A long exposition of

what in itself is simple implies imperfect understanding on the part of speaker or listener, writer or reader.

On se souvient du mot de St. Exupéry: "La perfection est atteinte non quand il n'y a plus rien à ajouter, mais quand il n'y a plus rien à retrancher." (i.e. "Perfection is attained, not when there is nothing more to be added, but when there is nothing more to be taken away.")*

Prosperity

Does not spiritual quality in man and woman exist in inverse ratio to acquired material prosperity?

In parts of the world in which poverty is still possible spiritual quality is more likely to be found than in parts of the world in which material prosperity has been imposed on the population.

It seems unlikely that material prosperity, sometimes termed a high standard of living, has any existence on the plane of Reality. Therefore as an aim in life it can have no spiritual significance.

Poverty has positive value in the eyes of men such as Saint Francis of Assisi, and material prosperity a negative value. Such also would seem to have been the belief of Jesus.

It seems unlikely, however, that the *attainment* of poverty has any greater significance than the *attainment* of prosperity. The material condition of a man (or woman), like the shape of his nose, may as well remain that with which he was born—as part of his normal background on the plane of Manifestation.

Materialists think of Rights rather than of Duties, yet it is the performance of duties rather than the exercise of rights

---

Ed. note: The above translation is not part of the original work.

that produces peace of mind, serenity, what is called happiness. Why? Perhaps because willingly to serve is a Positive action, to exact service a Negative action? But the acceptance of willing service is Positive, just as the performance of exacted service is Negative. Therein lies an adequate explanation of the misery of much that is contemporary life.

If acquired characters cannot be transmitted genetically, it is evident that they cannot be transmitted by what is called reincarnation either.

"You cannot judge another person unless you have seen and judged yourself": one mechanical being judging another mechanical being!

Humility of which one is conscious is not true humility. Virtue which is felt as such is not Virtue, though it may be correct action. On the intemporal plane there is Virtue: On the plane of manifestation there are virtues.

6 ·- *Reality and Manifestation - III*

What Did the Monk Realise When Overtaken by a So-called Satori-Experience?

The reality of anything is confined to the Instant, which we cannot normally seize and of which we only experience a reflection or an echo in the form of a memory.

Our mind is only a collection of reflections or echoes, preserved by memory, of the reality that we have missed. Our mind is merely a shadow which we mistake for the substance which we have never been able to see.

Perceiving the substance should be Satori. After seizing the Real, becoming Real, we realise that our mind was only a shadow—and that may be why the reaction was often a laugh. Past and Future vanish when the shaft of light falls upon the shadow, and only a Present, renewed every instant, remains, for that alone is real.

"We" are not the reality, not the substance, but its reflection. The substance is there, in Reality, hidden from us by the screen of Time. "We" are a shifting shadow on a wall, but the substance of that shadow is in every Instant that our consciousness is not able to seize. Our "life" on the plane of phenomena is a continuous misapprehension by which a reflection is mistaken for its image, an echo for its voice, a shadow for its substance.

We are phenomena, but we pretend to be noumena.

7 ·- Time and Space - III

The Screen of Time

Anyone, a child or a man partially blind, can poke a stick through a bicycle-wheel that is in repose. But when the wheel is in movement a stick will not pass. But if the movement of the stick were more rapid than the movement of the wheel, for instance if it were an arrow shot from a bow, it could pass.

Similarly anyone can throw a stone between the blades of an aeroplane propeller that is in repose, whereas if the propeller is in motion it will be rejected. But a bullet from a machine-gun, fired from behind the propeller, can pass, on account of its speed.

The spokes of the wheel, and the blades of the propeller, are clearly visible when they are not in movement or when the movement is slow, but as soon as the movement becomes rapid they become invisible. That is because the human eye does not react with a rapidity sufficient to seize the moving image. If the rapidity of reaction of the eye were increased, or the movement of the object retarded, the spokes or the blades again become visible. Artificially this can be done by means of photography, for the shutter of a camera can be operated at a greater velocity than the reaction of the human eye.

These common phenomena, and the so-called "laws" which appear to regulate them, may have a certain universality of application. In particular they may apply to our perception of Time. Phenomena are separated from noumena, or we from Reality, by the screen of Time. But this "screen," although a function of our own apparatus, should be like the "screen" formed by the revolving spokes or blades. If we could speed up our perception or slow down the apparatus we should be able to make contact with what is beyond.

But what is beyond? Undoubtedly what is beyond is a further dimension that is screened from us by our self-made time. Our whole lives are bounded by our time. Nowhere can we look, or perceive sensorially, without coming up against the limitation that is Time. But its frequency is too high for our senses to traverse. It seems just possible that the speed of light, regarded by Relativity as the ultimate velocity, may only be ultimate in the sense that we can experience no higher: and that because it may approach the velocity of Time itself, and so represent the frontier between our three sensorially perceptible dimensions and the next further. (The subjective character of Time cannot prevent it from having attributes.)

The "screen" in question is only impermeable in certain

conditions; as the term implies in science it is also the nature of a sieve. Just as many things, from light to bullets, can pass through the spoke and propeller "screens," so elements can pass through the "screen" of Time. One of these we sometimes term "intuition"; presumably because it has a higher frequency than thought it is able to pass. Reasoning is much slower, and the results obtained therewith are either false or have a degree of truth that is entirely relative.

In fact, however, everything of which we can have cognisance must have traversed our screen of Time, for on this side are phenomena and on the other is Noumenon. But such penetration is indirect. In the normal process of manifestation the "screen" has also the characteristics of a prism, a prism which splits up a motionless, colourless and formless unity, like light, into multiplicity and diversity.

A further example of the same phenomena is a simple apparatus called a phenakistoscope, in the form of a revolving cup with vertical slits in the side. On the inside of the cup is a series of designs in consecutive attitudes so that when the cup is revolved the illusion of movement is produced in anyone looking through the slits. This again is an effect of the insufficient rapidity of reaction of the human eye, the cinema-film being yet another. Were the ratio of the velocities to be readjusted—that of the eye augmented, that of the revolving cup reduced—the designs would be seen for what they are.

The purpose of this Note is to suggest that if a similar readjustment of frequencies were to take place in our consciousness—the rapidity of our perceptions increased, or that of our time-apparatus decreased—we should simply perceive Reality as it is!

8 ·– *Physics and Metaphysics - I*

Satori, 1

Satori is the absolute Present?

Is the *Satori-occurrence* anything but the seizure of the present, which henceforth gives that vision at right-angles which hitherto has been subjacent? And that is the *Satori-state*.

Zen is nothing but the realisation of Satori, but the understanding of Zen is not an idea in the mind: it is the mind itself.

All things considered, we cannot understand the ideas of others. We can only understand our own ideas.

The Zen masters did not seek to communicate knowledge. They consistently, and forcefully, refused to transfer concepts from their minds to those of their pupils. Their effort was confined to awakening direct cognition, and by means of action rather than by means of words.

Rejection of all that does not exist (in relative Reality), of all "let's pretend," of all political, social, and moral ideas, in favour of the aspect of Reality perceptible in manifestation— is the Zen masters' method of instruction. Religious, philosophic, and metaphysical notions received no greater consideration.

Prajna is the act of Action—pure perception, dynamic and concrete; an experience, not a concept.

The act of seeing is Prajna; recognition of the object seen is Vijnana. Absolute seeing, as opposed to partial or relative seeing, is Prajna.

The Satori-occurrence being the realisation that there is no I, there is no I to realise (to be self-conscious of) the Satori-occurrence.

And since there never was an I there can never have been a Satori-occurrence to abolish it, for neither ever existed in Reality. No wonder those who are assumed to have experienced it do not appear to be aware of the fact!

But the state of Satori, eternally existing, remains unaffected by this piece of illusionism.

9 ·~ Work and Play - II

Government

Democracy—rule by conflict of interests—is condemned to frustration by its own limitations. It can lead only to nullity.

To be creative, rule must be based not on conflict but on co-operation, not on interest but on disinterest, not on rights but on duties. Self-seeking and craftiness are poor instruments compared with sacrifice and service. Envy, hatred, malice, and all uncharitableness are negative and impotent, and no form of government which incites them could make a nation happy or prosperous.

Effective government can only come from above.

Health

It is less the medicine than the doctor that cures. It is less the doctor than the organic consciousness that heals. Always the organic consciousness is responsible for illness and for its cure. The doctor inspires, gives the impulsion that leads to health, the medicine helps or hinders locally to that end. Medicine-only is an attempt at healing *despite* the organic consciousness.

How may the organic consciousness be persuaded to re-establish balance, health (wholeness)? It is not a question of functional and nervous ailments more than of organic and lesional. When that is understood Lourdes will be understood, Jesus will be understood, healers of all techniques will be understood, and medicine will at last become rational, i.e. in accordance with relative reality, with the psycho-somatic entity as we can know it.

10 ·- Physics and Metaphysics - II

What Is Zen? 1

I do not know what answer learned persons give to this question, but personally I am at a loss each time that it is asked. I might reply, "Zen is the science of the realisation of our cosmic nature," but there are few questioners who would find that adequate.

So I will attempt a fuller definition, and see what happens.

History. Historically I believe Zen to be the philosophy of original Taoism, rendered immortal by the words attributed to Lao Tzu and Chuang Tzu, which proved to be too eclectic for the popular religion which Taoism became, but which, being a profound expression of relative truth, could not die and came to be absorbed by that very pure and *dépouillée* form of Buddhism said to have been introduced into China by Bodhidharma in the sixth century, and probably based on the Lankavatara sutra.

That form of Buddhism, traditionally the most authentic, comprehended by only a few, was termed DHYANA in Sanscrit, CH'AN in Chinese, and ZEN in Japanese. We are told that Dhyana means meditation, and this is repeated by all authorities despite the fact that meditation is continually condemned by the Masters of Zen and is in direct conflict with the way of life recommended by them. That Dhyana meant meditation in Sanscrit is presumably a fact, but what it meant, and still means, in China as CH'AN and in Japan as ZEN, is stated in the clearest and simplest possible manner by Hui Neng (Wei Lang) the sixth Patriarch from whom the modern doctrine directly descends. He states, in his sutra, "Dhyana means to be free from attachment to all outer objects," and again, "To be free from attachment to all outer objects is Dhyana." Nothing could be less ambiguous. If it is desirable to put it in different words one might say, "Dhyana means a state of mind unaffected by the field of sense-perceptions." What matters is what is meant by the word, not what the word meant in another language, at another period, in another land. It can be rendered in negative terms—Detachment, Non-identification, Non-reaction.

Object. Let me attempt to state what Zen is. I believe Zen to be a doctrine only in so far as it has an object and employs a method. Its object is the (necessarily instantaneous) realisation of a state of mind termed Satori in Japanese, Wu or Chienhsing in Chinese, and Sambhodi in Sanscrit, the most general English word for which may be Enlightenment. Many words are used in a similar context, but all are inadequate; for instance Liberation—but since there is nothing from which to be freed, except ignorance, the term is unfortunate. Terms such as Salvation, Nirvana, have a special context. "Realisation" alone ("of our cosmic nature" understood) is perhaps the best.

Method. The method by which this result is to be obtained may be defined as the elimination (by abolition or integration) of the artificial ego which has developed in the course of our lives as a result of our reactions to our surroundings. The reaction of the "me" to the "not-me" has produced an illusory entity, impermanent, ever-changing, whose apparent continuity is due to the circumstance of memory. As long as we suppose that this illusory entity, this phantasm, is "us" it remains impossible for any human being to realise his real, or original, nature which is one with the cosmos.

Technique. The technique whereby this elimination may be achieved consists in the attainment of non-attachment, complete detachment from values based on sense-impressions, such values being necessarily dualistic, constructed on a comparison of the opposites and thereby relative. No dualistic values—those according to which we normally conduct our lives—can have any existence in Reality. This technique is applied not by discipline but by understanding.

Characteristics. The Japanese have sought to make Zen the basis of a way of life, applying it to archery, swordsmanship, flower-arrangement, the tea-ceremony, and no doubt to other activities. It is also used as a religion (in the popular sense). But however satisfactory it may be in these adaptations its essential function is the realisation of the state of Satori (which has always existed in all of us) by means of the instantaneous Satori-occurrence. It is this or nothing. And if such be the aim of all forms of Buddhism (termed Nirvana), or of all religions (termed Salvation or otherwise) Zen represents the most direct method and the only one that rejects all dogma, all ritual, all devotion, and all belief. It might be regarded as the pure essence of religion.

The basis of its teaching is that from the beginning nothing phenomenal is, and that cosmic essence (Mind-only, Absolute Mind) is the only Reality.

Note: It is suggested above that the term "Liberation" is unfortunate, because no one has put us in prison; on the other hand, since liberation from an unreal ego is the essential fact of Zen and constitutes Satori, it can equally be considered precise and accurate. It depends on what the term suggests to whoever uses it.

Satori, 2 (referring to *Satori, 1*, p. 21)

On the other hand, if Satori be regarded as the realisation that the "I" is all-and-everything—which is the same thing looked at from another point of view—the "I" should disappear as consciousness of an entity, and the Satori-occurrence which released that realisation would disappear with it.

Both concepts are probably necessary to a full understanding.

If Satori is access to a further dimension, then the opposites should be transcended therein, since the splitting into opposites is the effect of the screen or prism of Time (which is the limitation of perceived dimensions).

From the second dimension the first becomes observable in its entirety. From the third (height or depth) the first and second (a plane surface) become observable in their entirety. It follows that from a fourth dimension (another right-angle to all other dimensions) the first three (a volume) are observable in their entirety. Therefore if Satori is access to that further dimension perception therefrom includes all things. This is surely another way of describing the metaphysical concept that Satori is a realisation that the "I" is all-and-everything.

Expressed differently: the second dimension, being infinite repetition of the first at right-angles, contains the first an infinite number of times within itself. The third dimension, being infinite repetition of the two first at right-angles to them, contains them (a surface) an infinite number of times within itself. Therefore a fourth dimension, being an infinite repetition of volume at right-angles thereto, contains that an infinite number of times within itself.

If Satori represents access to that fourth dimension then the "I" that perceives must automatically realise that it includes within itself all-and-everything.

Note: When it is pointed out that from a fourth dimension a volume becomes observable in its entirety—that means that it becomes observable also from what we regard as "within."

Dimensions have been regarded above as if they formed part of the structure of an external reality. Regarded as analytical elements of the human mind the result will be found to be the same though the concept will be considerably more difficult.

❧

In regarding Realisation as a personal phenomenon, if not attainment, are we not making a fundamental and disastrous error? Surely Realisation is impersonal—*the realisation of our basic impersonality?*

11 ∙ Time and Space - IV

La Vida Es Sueño

Tridimensional manifestation seems to be the splitting up of Reality into relative appearances, like light through a prism, or a physical object seen through an optical instrument composed of planes, screens and lenses; but our senses perceive that Reality as the ten-thousand-things which are merely projections of Reality, not Reality itself. The "prism" or optical instrument is in our own receptive apparatus and is known as Time.

This concept—and we can only reason in concepts—seems to cover the multifarious teachings of the Masters and to render them conceivable, but it remains no more than an image and cannot be regarded as a statement of objective fact even considered on the relative plane.

Perhaps, however, if we are able to conceive "ourselves" as projections which we have been mistaking for reality, we should be nearer to an understanding which should open the way to the desired intuitional cognition that transcends all concepts.

The human being may be no more real than is a cinematograph film. When the projected light is switched off all that remains is a blank screen. That which has been projected by light was a series of "stills." Such also is what is being projected by "life." The more you consider the analogy the more perfect it seems to be: it could help us to understand.

Direct Perception

Every sense-perception is in itself instantaneous, spontaneous, and impersonal. It is in the Present, is the Present, the only Present we ever know. But as soon as we recognise the object as perceived by us the subject, intellection has taken place, and it belongs to the Past—for the intellect only operates on what is already passed. Living it came; seized upon by the mind, it lives no longer, for the intellect only feeds on dead meat.

The act of cognition slays the living perception. Were it otherwise the incident, or lack of incident, would be what is known as Satori.

❦

Intuition appears to be high-frequency thought that can pass through the screen of Time. If density is a function of frequency Satori may be a raising of the mental processes to a frequency that gives access to a further dimension.

The Kingdom of Heaven Is Within

We live entirely on surfaces, and everything we do is superficial. However deeply we cut into anything, dig into the earth, or however much we break up any material object, we never find anything but surfaces.

From birth to death we never see the inside of anything, for whatever we do, and whichever way we turn, our senses are met by surfaces.

For surfaces are tridimensional, as are our senses and no doubt as a result of our senses. The fourth dimension is within. Inside anything is the fourth dimension. The fourth dimension is ubiquitous, it is omnipresent, immanent, it is not something speculative, an unnecessary conjecture, a dubious theory: every portion of everything that exists, or appears to exist, must have an in-side as well as an out-side, and the fourth dimension is that in-side of everything that we know.

Besides, where does everything "come from"? Trees do not grow from nowhere. All growth, all development, all coming-into-manifestation is surely from where the subject is but from a dimension that we are not able to perceive sensorially.

Symbols

One may suspect that symbols are essentially quadridimensional. They may represent the "within" of ideas. That may be an element in the explanation of the symbolic character of dreams—for psychologists have found dreams to be essentially symbolic. It may also explain the power attributed to symbols in all forms of esotericism.

The notion that there are only three dimensions is primitive. In fact we only know how to make use of three. In any case a dimension is not a thing-in-itself: it is an intellectual instrument. There are as many as we care to use, as many as we may need. The fourth exists neither more nor less than the second. Their purpose is to help us to understand the phenomenal universe which surrounds us and of which we are a part. As long as we limit them to three we are able to understand at most the physical part of our being and the outside of everything that is accessible to our senses.

A dimension can never be anything but a mathematical concept.

Movement Is Within

If life were to stop for a perceptible moment it would cease to be life; but it would be Time that had stopped. Therefore Time is Movement. But Time is within ourselves ("a function of our receptive apparatus"—Kant); therefore Movement is within ourselves.

When we stop (die) Movement stops, and life remains immobile, i.e. eternal—in its permanent state. Do we realise the implications of this?

12 ·- *Physics and Metaphysics - III*

What Is Zen? 2

The essentials of the doctrine known to us as Zen antedate Buddhism. They are implicit in Lao Tzu, who was a contemporary of the Buddha in the Far East, and they are explicit in Chuang Tzu a couple of generations later. The Tao Te Ching was not the annunciation of a new doctrine, but a commentary on a teaching already ancient.

Zen doctrine has come down to us in a Buddhist context and it is impregnated with the teaching of the Buddha. Even if the traditional origin of the Flower Sermon could be regarded as authentic the Chinese element has an independent origin in the original Taoism.

❧

Has no materialist ever suggested that Zen is the *reductio ad absurdum* of Buddhism? If not, why not?

❧

The Void of Buddhism becomes more readily understandable if it may be regarded as meaning that which is void of qualities, evaluations projected by the dualistic human mind.

13 ·‒ *Reality and Manifestation - IV*

One cannot get rid of one's apparent ego by throwing stones at it as if it were an importunate cur. It will only go when one comes to understand that it isn't there.

Dreams

Swami Siddheswarananda points out that when we dream we perceive ourselves doing something. This dream-ego thinks he perceives what appears to be taking place, but it is really We who perceive both the dream-ego and what appears to be taking place. The dream-ego is a part of the scenario, of what appears to be happening, of the dream, and is neither more nor less real than any other element therein.

Our waking-ego is no different. Our waking ego thinks he perceives everything that appears to be taking place, and attributes to himself the independent position of spectator, but he too is merely a part of what appears to be happening, of the scenario of daily life, and is neither more nor less real than any other element therein.

It is only the real "I" that is the Spectator, and that "I" is intemporal.

We imagine that waking-life is real and that dream-life is unreal, but there does not seem to be any evidence for this belief. Chuang Tzu, in the third century B.C., put it in an amusing way; having dreamed that he was a butterfly flitting from flower to flower, he stated that he was now wondering whether he was then a man dreaming he was a butterfly or whether he was now a butterfly dreaming he was a man.

Does it not seem that of the two experiences dream-life is likely to contain more of reality than waking-life? Dream-life appears to be quadridimensional whereas waking-life is only tridimensional. The apparent oddity of dream-life to the waking mind (it does not appear odd to the dreamer) is probably due to the fact that the dream has to be translated into tridimensional terms in order to be remembered—and usually only bits are translated. We can only remember tridimensionally. As far as can be judged, both experiences appear equally real when they are taking place.

The outstanding psychologists have laid bare the symbolic character of dreams, but they can only interpret what they have understood in tridimensional terminology: it could never be possible to restore to a dream its original quadridimensional nature, for we have no means of conceiving that nature with the mechanism of our three-dimensional minds.

The Indian philosophers looked to dreamless sleep to find a contact with Reality, but there does not appear to be any evidence that such a state in fact exists or is other than a metaphysical concept. Is it indeed necessary to posit such a state? May not the normal dream-state, as we live it and not as we subsequently interpret it, imply contact with a much less relative reality than any we know, if not with Reality itself?

Leaving aside this dualistic approach; from the point of view of unicity the Spectator and the Spectacle, the dream-world, the waking-world, and the observer thereof, are one and the same. Perhaps one might say that they may be regarded as the Spectator looking at Himself analytically.

Aspects of Not-Being, 2

Dr. Herbert Benoit explains that there is no more reason to suppose that we choose a cravat than there is to suppose that it is the cravat that chooses us. Although this statement strikes some people as amusing and original it is, in fact, implicit in our normal habit of speech. Who does not say, "I was attracted by that cravat"? But in that encounter the speaker was the passive element and the cravat the active: the cravat exercised attraction and the speaker suffered attraction. In short the cravat chose the speaker.

To say "This tie chose me" is to say the same thing as "This tie attracted me," but to say, "This tie bought me" is to introduce an operation in which the tie did not in fact actively participate. Were I to say to a waiter, sitting down to dinner in a restaurant, "I want to be eaten by a spring-chicken this evening," a similar incongruity would be introduced although the same essential truth would underlie it.

Such statements are sometimes considered to be "Zen," but one may wonder whether there is any necessary connection between Zen and paradox.

Action and Non-Action, 2

"Mad monkeys." It is said in the East that "La maladie des occidentaux est le travail." We may prefer to say that superfluous activity is the sickness of the West. For, all things

considered, a very great proportion of what we call "work" is ultimately unnecessary.

We are obsessed with the importance of Doing, much of which goes by the name of "work"—somewhat euphemistically no doubt. This obsession has been increasing in intensity for many decades, and now is an *article de foi*. It is taken as a matter of course that everyone must "do" something always and all the time. It is regarded as a virtue, and its non-observance as a vice. The average person, without thinking (for he rarely thinks of such things), attributes merit to his fellows, and particularly to the young, in ratio to their activity. But at least fifty percent of the activities in question are futile even to us and probably about nine-tenths are, *ultimately considered*, superfluous. It is doubtful if more than a very small percentage are either fundamentally necessary or beneficial.

For Doing is an avoidance, an escape, a running-away from Reality.

Such a statement will seem outrageous to the present generation, but one can safely say that it would appear a platitude to Lao Tzu if he should happen to read it.

This attitude of the present generation is based on the tacit assumption that material things are not only real but beneficial. If one should be able to perceive that they are neither—the view of Lao Tzu will rapidly become obvious.

To the average man or woman there is no alternative to Doing but Idleness. If that were so it might be difficult to decide which of the alternatives should be preferred. Since both are probably futile there may be nothing to choose between them, although Idleness would seem to be relatively innocuous.

But should not the alternative to Doing rather be regarded as Being?

Metaphysically this appears to be a ternary proposition: the opposites, Doing and Idleness, achieving their synthesis in Being. Being is the apex of the triangle wherein the dualistic bases, Doing and Idleness, become absorbed in Unicity. Behind Action and Inaction lies Non-Action, which manifests in them.

But normally we do not know how to Be. If we did know how to Be all our activity would be necessary action (work in its pure sense) and all our passivity would be not idleness but dynamic inaction.

The sensation approaching terror that modern men and women experience when faced with the possibility of having nothing to "do" is probably a fear of finding nothing between their relative ego and their real ego which is absolute. Doing—work and distraction (distraction from what?)—constitute a screen between the apparent "I" and the real "I." Were they to come face to face with the latter the whole false facade of their illusory personality would collapse like a house of cards, they would be naked and humbled, conscious of their nullity—and they are unprepared to understand that therein lies serenity and liberation. The apparent void is a plenitude.

The concept just referred to as the relative ego and placed in opposition to the real ego is open to criticism from several angles, but there is as yet no exact terminology in these matters. Indeed exact terminology in the expression of that which cannot be expressed will always be difficult. Truth, when expressed, thereby ceases to be truth, and Reality can only be distorted into words.

In the first place there is only the real ego, and that is

universal Mind, the relative ego being a distorted aspect of that. In the second place the relative ego is a percept of which the average man or woman is only aware as the nucleus round which has gathered the perfectly illusory complex of his or her personality. The relative ego, a pure percept like any other "thing," is representative of a segment, of part of a whole, and devoid of any kind of evaluation. What a man regards as his ego is his interpretation of that, based on his collection of memories of reactions to his environment, no longer a percept but an affective concept, a false evaluation (false because an evaluation) that is entirely illusory.

It is in order to sustain this illusory complex, that he thinks is "himself," that he feels obliged eternally to "do" and to urge others to "do," that is to behave as what the orientals refer to as a "mad monkey," and it is from fear of the destruction of this illusory personality that he dare not face up to his real self in silence and the awareness of Being.

Note: Relative reality is only metaphorically "distorted": less inaccurately it might be described as an unrepresentative fragment, segment, or deputy. Call it a stooge if you will. A formal representation of the Informal might be likened to an algebraic sign—which represents something that it in no way resembles.

Reality and the Ego, 2

Referring to the first note on *Reality and the Ego* (Ch. 3) it might be worth while pointing out that in more technical language political, ethical, and social notions are in fact interpretive evaluations, similar to those that constitute the illusory aspect of our relative ego. "Things in themselves," i.e. relative reality, are pure precepts, but as soon as we attribute qualities to them, evaluate them, they become affective concepts and as such are perfectly illusory.

❧

Cause and effect may not be two things separated in time but one whole thing in reality.

Neither Subjective Nor Objective

It has been pointed out above that the ego is not the Spectator of the Spectacle, but can there be a Spectacle without a Spectator to make it a spectacle?

If there is no "I" there is no observer, but can there be an observed? Logically there cannot be an observer without something observed, nor something observed without an observer.

There can be no Subject without an Object, nor an Object without a Subject, for each depends upon (is relative to) the other and exists as a function of the other.

In Reality the two are one. And so they are said to become in realisation. That would seem to be what is meant by passing beyond subjectivity and objectivity.

The Phenomenal Self and the Illusory Self

A man without a false-ego would be like a hedgehog without bristles, but a man without an ego would be like a log of wood or a jellyfish—if he did not simply fall to pieces.

Every conscious being must have an ego. Every unity has a centre, its rallying-point; the solar system and the atom have their nuclei, around which their elements are grouped. Far from being something superfluous, of which we should rid ourselves, it is the essential factor of the organism, as the heart is of the physical body.

When one attacks the "egoism" of somebody one is guilty of a misuse of words: it is not his ego that is insufferable but his "illusory self." The ego belongs to so-called relative-Reality. It may be masked by the fictitious "me," but itself is a functional necessity.

The ego, or nucleus of centrifugal and centripetal forces, which should be regarded as an aspect of Reality, can be the subject of pure, instantaneous perception, but the interpretation that our mind gives to this perception transforms it into an element of the illusory self.

"The Tathagata Declares That Characteristics Are Not Characteristics" (Diamond Sutra XIV)

Is Humility anything but the result of a diminution of the power of the fictitious-self? Is it not in fact a function of the degree of consciousness, or of the sensation, of self?

This being so, it does not exist as a quality: it is only an evaluation.

To seek humility as a thing-in-itself is absurd.

All forms of discipline, oriental (yoga) or occidental, only attack symptoms and could only have a superficial and temporary effect—like a febrifuge against typhoid-fever.

Our spiritual misery has but one basis, and there is only one treatment for it: its cause is the illusory self, and the treatment consists in realising that that does not exist.

However, intellectual recognition is not enough.

After all, the "me" is our own creation; it is not imposed upon us from without; it is created by our reactions to everything that happens to us.

Reality and Relativity

The expression "Relative-Reality," although accepted, appears to be nonsense. How could Reality be relative? By definition it is unconditioned. That being so, it would seem better squarely to accept the contradiction and to speak, rather, of "conditioned Reality."

The element of relativity applies to our interpretation and to nothing else. Our perception or our comprehension of Reality (as of everything) can be relative, but not the object of our perception or of our comprehension.

We can have a pure perception of an aspect of Reality, of a partial, that is to say phenomenal, presentation of Reality, but we cannot perceive either Reality Itself or any reality relative to It.

Reality does not admit of an adjective. Even "phenomenal Reality" is nonsense. There can only be a "phenomenal aspect of Reality." The composite term "Reality-phenomenon," meaning "Reality perceived as phenomenon," alone seems to be adequate, but, for those who understand, the word "Reality" here is already superfluous.

Ouspensky

As Ouspensky tells us: on the noumenal plane, the plane of Reality, multi-dimensional, Time exists spatially, and temporal events exist—they don't happen. "Effects" co-exist with their "causes," and moments of different epochs exist simultaneously and contiguously. Points far apart in tridimensional space can touch one another, proximity and separation become affinity and repulsion, sympathy and antipathy. There is neither matter nor movement. Nothing is dead, nothing is unconscious. If that is what he said, need he have said anything else?

14 ·– Work and Play - III

Work as Service

That unique monument of Indian wisdom, the *Bhagavad Gita*, has much to tell us about the nature of action, which is no doubt a measure of the importance of the subject.

"The world is imprisoned in its own activity," we are told, "except when actions are performed as worship of God." This is not the Buddhist approach, but it is an expression of the truth which should be all the easier for Christians. "Therefore you must perform every action sacramentally, and be free from all attachment to results." Nothing could be clearer, unless the following:

"You have the right to work, but for the work's sake only. You have no right to the fruits of work. Desire for the fruits of work must never be your motive in working."

"They who work selfishly for results are miserable."

To most modern men and women this is not merely unacceptable—it is incomprehensible. But many of these Notes are in that category, and the truth of these words is patent to those who are able to see. The modern man works not only for results, in most cases he works for what he can earn thereby. So far has he gone to the opposite extreme to that set forth in the *Gita* that he sometimes even persuades himself that he has no right to work unless he is paid for it. Full payment for work of any kind, for service of any kind, has acquired a character that is almost sacramental, i.e. not the work but the remuneration has now that character. The obvious fallacy of this attitude is obscured by dogma and propaganda, which, as we know, *ipso facto* cannot be true.

But what does the *Gita* mean when its words are applied to modern life?

That most men must live by their work is not in itself a justification of the current view. Supposing we put the case like this: that men should be remunerated according to the status, the degree of resposibility, of the work they are able to do, in order that they may live worthily in accordance with that status or responsibility, but that the remuneration they receive should be for their living and not for their work? Supposing, moreover, that they should receive it as for their living, and that their work should be a service—what the *Gita* would call a sacrament?

Let us remember that it is not such a conception as this that is new—though it may seem so to a modern man; this conception, indeed, is normal and older than the *Gita* itself, as old as human civilisation. As recently as the end of the last century, not to mention many isolated cases still surviving today, not only men in exhalted and responsible positions were so remunerated and worked as a service, but also men and women in ordinary domestic employment. In both cases, as the basis of the contract, their lives were protected, they were cared for, they received housing, food, sometimes clothing, and money for their personal needs. In return they were given the opportunity of service. Sometimes the service called for was intensive, to the limit of their capacity, at other times it was little more than a formality—but their remuneration was in no way affected thereby or dependent on what they did. So it has been in all walks of life throughout history.

Such an age-old principle is basically different from that which seeks payment for each hour's work, which demands as much as can be extorted and gives as little as possible in return.

Yet in that way happiness is possible and a life that is worthy of a self-respecting human being. In that way man is free to develop spiritually; in the other there is only misery and degradation. That surely is what the *Gita* means—applied to daily life: "They who work selfishly for results are miserable." We have only to look around us in order to see.

It may be objected that such a principle is inapplicable to industrial organisation, but we are considering something more fundamental than that; the being of man and his use of his mind may be sacrosanct—industrial organisation certainly is not. We are considering the development of understanding and calling upon the eternal wisdom of the Song of God to aid us, which wisdom is never in conflict with that of the Lord Buddha, the Lord Jesus, or the supremely wise men of any age or place. Man may be essentially divine, but there is nothing holy about his commercial activities. Just as laws are made for man, not man for laws (a circumstance apt to be overlooked by some people) so commerce was made for man, not man for commerce (a circumstance not merely overlooked but contraverted).

Men could abuse such a system of service, and did, but that did not matter. Some gave what the modern man would call too much (though that is probably impossible), and others too little; it was they, primarily, who benefited—in the former case, and suffered—in the latter.

Work should be a sacrament, according to the *Gita*. Work should be a service, we may prefer to say. What is certain is that people should not be bribed to work, should not consider their "rights" (have we any?) except in relation to their duties, and should not take except in the certainty of giving more than they receive.

I cannot leave the *Bhagavad Gita* without quoting these few words:

"There never was a time," says Sri Krishna, "when I did not exist, nor you . . . nor is there any future in which we shall cease to be."

These words do not seem to call for exposition. If they need explanation that is to be found in these Notes in so far as I may be capable of giving it.

"That which is non-existent," Sri Krishna says again, "can never come into being, and that which is can never cease to be."

15 ·- Reality and Manifestation – V

"Transcending the Self"—Which?

It seems to be evident that we must conceive (*a*) an absolute-Self, which is the Absolute, which is one with the cosmic Essence, universal Mind (to bring together most of the usual terms), the noumenal Self which may be conceived as the personal aspect of the Absolute.

(*b*) Then a relative, or conditioned, Self—which is the manifested Self, the phenomenal Self, the "individual," the incarnate Self, with its limited consciousness, its hereditary body and its psyche or mind, and which is part of all the phenomenal manifestations of the Absolute, of Reality. It is our centre, our nucleus round which "we" (all the elements which our false perspective sees as one) are grouped.

(*c*) Finally there are the artificial "me's," fictitious, products without substance, of our mental activities, imaginary things, complexes, without permanence, changing, mechanical, living on psychic tensions, with which we falsely identify ourselves, and which dominate us by means of the affirmations and negations that they require of us and that we spend our whole lives in providing for.

It is these last that we have to transcend, that are the basis of our suffering.

Once we have eliminated these false "me's," these illusory "selves," these mirages in which we see, feel, think, live, the way will be open towards our full evolution. As long as we remain subject to the illusion of their reality, identified with them, we cannot evolve. The saint himself, by disciplining these "me's," by rendering them positive instead of negative, cannot evolve. Only the Sage, who has understood, who eliminates them by understanding that they do not really exist, can come to obtain a glimpse of his veritable nature and, ultimately, become *himself*.

Note: When someone speaks to us of the "me," the "ego," the "self," of the "personality," the "individual," the "being," with capital letters or lower case, it is often difficult to know what is in question; it may be (*a*), (*b*), or (*c*), or a mixture of the three—nearly always a mixture of (*b*) and of (*c*).

Nevertheless (*a*) alone is real, (*b*) alone is relative, (*c*) alone is fictitious or illusory. It matters little which word is chosen provided it be specified or implied that it is a question of the "me," "I," "self," "personality," "ego," "being"—that is absolute, relative (conditioned), or fictitious. Otherwise never can the word itself suffice.

At the same time it is not a question of three different things, nor of three degrees of one and the same thing—for there are no "things." The relative-self represents a manifestation on the plane of phenomena of the Absolute-Self (the Self of all things)—of the Absolute manifesting, or perceived, as self, whereas the fictitious "me"s are transient mirages manufactured by the apparatus which is a part of the relative self.

Ultimately they are concepts rendered necessary in order that we may understand something; and it would be an error to suppose that any one of them really exists.

The Illusion of Continuous Individuality

The fact that everything is renewed every moment constitutes the *mechanism* of the change that may be observed. It represents the reality behind the apparent impermanence of all things.

Memory alone seems to justify our idea of continuity, our impression of being the same individual from our birth until our death rather than a series of innumerable individuals, each resembling the other but each one different, in the end giving the impression of gradual change; so that this faculty of memory would seem to be the least illusory element in our "self." We can claim that alone as being truly ourselves. Our notion of continuity has no other basis.

The Saint is a man who disciplines his ego. The Sage is a man who rids himself of his ego.

The Saint retains the illusion of a "me" and lives inside his mirage. The Sage walks through this mirage and finds that there was no "me" in reality.

Matter is probably a function and is not a thing-in-itself. We are in error in regarding substance as a real thing: it is probably a density of cosmic energy.

Walking through the Mirage

When the artificial "I" is left behind, the real "I" that remains perceives directly instead of through the refracting and muddy waters of the false "I." The "scent of the wild laurel," the "cypress tree in the courtyard," the cup of tea, the "when I'm hungry I eat, when I'm thirsty I drink, when I'm tired I lie down," the "nothing is hidden from you," of the Zen Masters are the straight-seeing. It is the water freed from the ice that held it frozen. But it is only looking straight out of your eyes, it is nothing far off, mysterious, out of touch, imperceptible at present: *it is what is there now.*

It is We-as-we-are, with our smoked glasses put aside.

There can be no attainment in Realisation, because an I is necessary in order to attain.

Realisation being the realisation that there is no I—there is no I to attain and nothing can have been attained.

But is not an I necessary in order to realise that there is no I? How then can there be Realisation?

Memory may be regarded as the cement of the ego.

16 ⁓ Physics and Metaphysics – IV

What Is Zen? 3

Hui Hai, quoting the "Sutra of Reflections on Progress" says: "If in all matters he permits himself no attachment, that is called (practising) the *dhyana paramita*, or meditation."

That may not be our idea of "meditation"—but that is evidently what the word means as a translation of "dhyana," for the essential meaning of non-attachment is therein.

Later he says: "No-attachment means that feelings of hatred and love do not arise. That is what is meant by no attachment."

Our words, as translated, do not necessarily mean to us what the Sanscrit and Chinese words meant to them.

Is it clear that the term "Zen" (Dhyana, Ch'an) does *not* mean what we mean by meditation? (See *Physics and Metaphysics – II*, Ch. 10)

Satori, 3

It seems clear that when the four-dimensional consciousness (Wu hsin—the Zen No-Mind) is attained the mutually conditioned evaluations (the so-called pairs of opposites or complementaries) disappear (are no longer seen as such).

Since our reasoning is based on the primitive process of a comparison of these relative evaluations it should follow that the logic of the quadridimensional mind is different from the logic of the tridimensional mind.

If this does not in fact explain the strange statements of the Zen masters in their "mondo" it provides at least a key to the situation in which such statements arise.

The Unconscious (in Zen, not the psychology of the false

ego), Mind-only, and Universal Mind, may all be attempts to indicate what is really just the fourth dimension of mind. That the Zen "Unconscious" is that seems to be fairly obvious: but the identification between that and Mind-only, which, however, Professor Suzuki makes*, is less easy to perceive.

As phenomena we are an expression of a quadridimensional noumenon?

No Merit Whatsoever

All generosity that is conscious and affective (any gesture, kindness, charity, or gift) is as much an affirmation and reinforcement of the false "me" as any maleficence (spitefulness, expression of envy, hatred, greed, malice). That was demonstrated by Bodhidharma's devastating reply to the pious emperor—"No merit whatsoever, your Majesty."

We may know that, but do we understand it? The man who has transcended his artificial ego would no longer distinguish his own needs from those of others, and would not think of them more or less readily. Anything he might do for others would occasion a reaction no different from that caused by anything he did for himself. All should be pure *Caritas***, limpid and impersonal.

---

* *Ed. note:* W. W. W. may be referring here to Suzuki's discussion of Zen and "the Unconscious" in *The Zen Doctrine of No Mind,* pp. 57-68.
** *Ed. Note:* W. W. W. uses this Greek word in its original meaning of "pure, impersonal compassion."

17 · Time and Space - V

The Scale of Observation Creates the Phenomenon

Phenomena only appear to us as they do as a result of the focal range at which they are placed in relation to our sense organs. At another focal range we should perceive galaxies of atoms and their satellites where now we perceive what we describe as a tea-cup. At the closer focal range no independent forms, no separate phenomena would be perceptible, or knowable even by inference. At a longer focal range they would again become indistinguishable. Even in physics Form and Substance are dependent on a physical adjustment, and only exist subject to an artificial arrangement of our sensorial apparatus.

❧

If Cause and Effect are one whole thing in Reality—the effect being the obverse of the cause, then, since no Effect has a single Cause in Space-Time, a vast linkage emerges, Time and Space close up like a concertina, and assume the appearance (in thought) of a solid motionless block.

Reincarnation and Recurrence, 2

In reality there are no living beings to be liberated by the Tathagata.
> —The Buddha, in the Diamond Sutra XXV

"Rebirth" could be the result of dying without having transcended the three dimensions plus time (dying with the fourth dimension still perceived as time).

So dying the event of death would not relieve us of that limitation and our consciousness might have to continue (as far as it itself was concerned) subject to that illusion—*which in itself constitutes what we know as life.* But since consciousness is based on memory, and since memory is not "re-born" (carried over from birth to birth), what would be left to reincarnate apart from the capacity for awareness?

The four-dimensional consciousness once realised, we live out our "lives" but we could not be "reborn."

When there is no longer time (no Past or Future), i.e. once our "life" is over, having *realised* that "time" is non-existent as such and is only the fourth dimension of space—how could there be re-birth?

"Life" is itself an illusion, i.e. the process of "living" is not real. The Diamond Sutra tells us that, and, perhaps, little else.

18 ·- *Reality and Manifestation - VI*

Dualism

The non-dual nature=the true nature=The Essence of Mind=the Tao.

Every single thing can only claim to exist as a function of its opposite; therefore they cannot claim to be two things: they can only be two ways of looking at one thing.

Every so-called pair of opposites (or complementaries) are really one.

Being cannot exist except as a function of Non-being, Self as a function of Not-self (but for the existence of Non-being and Not-self neither Being nor Self could so be). "I am Not-I, therefore I am I."

Therefore everything that is or could be is both itself and

its opposite (or complementary).

Each of every pair of opposites is the reciprocal cause of the other; all opposites are the reciprocal cause of one another.

We have heard about that before somewhere? Assuredly. But have we understood it?

"Like an image seen in a mirror, which is not real, the Mind is seen by the ignorant in a dualistic form in the mirror of habit-energy" (Lanka, LXXIV). "Habit-energy" appears to be a wholly admirable way of describing memory.

This may mean that we perceive everything non-dualistically (that all pure perceptions are in unicity), but that when our perceptions become conscious, being then *interpretations of a memory,* they appear dualistically.

If that be so we have only to perceive directly in order to realise unicity. But can our perceptions ever have the necessary instantaneity for that?

ॐ

The limited consciousness is subject to, perhaps feeds on, continual attraction and repulsion. That may be the heart of the matter.

Reality and the Ego, 3

It is only the artificial ego that suffers. The man who has transcended his false "me" no longer identifies himself with his suffering.

The constituents of the "me" exist as evaluations, interpretations: it is the notion, by means of identification, that this constitutes an entity, that is illusory.

Pride and Humility are functions of the false ego.

Humility which is conscious is an aspect of Pride and affirms the false ego. When the false ego is reduced the absence of pride (which was reduced *pro rata* with that of which it was merely a manifestation) may have the appearance of humility, but the subject is unconscious thereof, it is not really present, its appearance is an effect of contrast with past Pride. The subject is now merely himself.

"In utter stillness (of the mind) the ego does not exist" (Hui Hai, p. 39).

The Only Truth

If we try to interpret the concept whereby there is nothing but Mind (Mind-only, Universal-Mind, etc.) as a primary substance underlying the atom—as pure energy, for instance, we may be looking diametrically in the wrong direction. For such a way of looking is objective and dualistic, involving observer and observed. Mind (of Mind-only, Universal-Mind) is consciousness rather—the ultimate Within. We are not either Without or Within Mind-only: it is within us only because it is us and we are it.

"The world which is mind-manifested," as the Lankavatara Sutra puts it, "is stirred up by the wind of objectivity, it evolves and dissolves," i.e. it is of us and we are of it.

Words could never express what that is: they can only suggest. It may not be possible to get nearer.

Comment on the Essential Doctrine of the Lankavatara Sutra

". . . recognition of the truth that an external world is nothing but the Mind itself." (Lanka, LVIII)

"As they are tenaciously clinging to the thought of an

53

ego-soul and all that belongs to it, they are really unable to understand what is meant by the doctrine of Mind-only." (Lanka LXXI)

The full concept involves a combination of what has just been said, i.e. that nothing exists outside the Mind, with the non-entity of any kind of ego. Since the act of conceiving such a concept implies an entity to perform such an act of conceiving, such act would appear to be impossible. Therefore it cannot be a concept but an abstract and inexpressible state of pure knowledge.

"There is an exalted *state of inner attainment* which does not fall into the dualism of oneness and otherness . . . which has nothing to do with logic, reasoning, theorising, and illustrating . . . this I call self-realisation." (The Buddha in Lanka, LXXII)

Therefore the Sutras, the doctrines, *all teachings,* are only a means.

"I have two forms of teaching the truth: self-realisation and discoursing. I discourse with the ignorant and disclose self-realisation to the yogins (the wise)." (The Buddha in Lanka, LXXII)

"Where perfect knowledge is, there is nothing (dualistically) existent." (Lanka, LV)

"And when he thus recognises *the non-existence of the external world, which is no more than his own mind,* he is said to

have the will-body." (Lanka, LVII)

Or, as we would put it—Nothing exists outside the Mind. When so plainly stated it is worth extracting.

"The ignorant are delighted with discoursing . . . discoursing is a source of suffering in the triple world." (Lanka, LXXIV)
Indeed one has suspected that.

The primary trouble with us, particularly those of us who write, is that we know too much and understand too little.

Perhaps we think too much, read too much, talk too much, write too much—and are still too rarely? The only opportunity we leave ourselves of understanding may be when we are asleep?

The mind seems to be a machine for the production of phenomena, which it projects from within itself much as does a cinematograph projector.

"With the birth of the mind every kind of phenomenon is produced. With the destruction of the mind every kind of phenomenon is destroyed." (Hui Hai, quoting the Lanka)
Could anything be clearer?

Freewill and Reality

Our reactions are our own, and free; our actions are determined—their apparent freedom is illusory.

Owing to our conditioning we have the illusion that our actions are free, that is we are unable to avoid behaving as though we had freedom of choice in our behaviour. But we are not constrained to believe in this apparent liberty in the execution of our will. We observe that we can often do as we will, but we have no reason to suppose that we can influence that will. Presumably that will itself is subject to determination the mechanism of which we are unable to perceive.

Just as we are apt to believe that our actions are free, so we tend to suppose that our reactions are determined, since we feel unable to control them. At most we recognise a power of suppression, but that is not control.

Since the ego is the subject of these processes the ego is unfree. As long as we remain identified with the ego we remain unfree—purely mechanical beings reacting to stimuli, as Gurdjieff said. It follows that in so far as we become detached from the illusory ego to that degree we attain freedom to act as we will.

But such freedom is not the arbitrary exercise of caprice that the term suggests according to our normal manner of reasoning. The Jivan Mukta, the man of satori, he who has transcended his ego, does not act as a result of choice: he acts as he must, intuitively as we call it, without reasoning, in accordance with cosmic necessity, and his action is always correct (or adequate) action.

That alone is Freedom of will in terms of Reality.

People who cannot make up their minds usually wish to do something that they are unable to will.

They have perhaps a conflict of desires, of wishes of the artificial personality, none of which can they will—for the will can only act in conformity with karmic necessity. Consequently they shilly-shally until the will itself comes into operation—and then they do what they must. On the other hand people who "know what they want," people of instant decision, are people who are deaf to the clamour of the false "me" and who accept the dictates of their will at once and do that which has to be done in any case.

It is possible to silence the clamour of the false ego; instead of consulting it, to ignore it, and to let the will speak. (But in common parlance the term "will" is often used to designate the executive aspect of desire.)

❧

We ourselves are not an illusory part of Reality; rather are we Reality itself illusorily conceived.

The man of satori does as he must (in accordance with cosmic necessity). So do we. The only difference is that we go through the pantomime, or illusory process, of reasoning about it whereas he just acts.

"What we must do" is not necessarily nor to any recognisable extent coincident with what we desire, with what we regard as advantageous or affirmative of our ego.

If we observe a spin of a roulette-wheel and seek to allow our Mind to tell us what number or colour will turn up we have the idea of utilising for our own benefit (or at least of utilising) any intuition so obtained. But that we are unable to do, and must be unable to do. Between the answer regarding what we must do and the answer regarding what will turn up there is no necessary connection whatever.

We may learn to know what we must do, but we should avoid the error of supposing that such action will have any bearing on what we desire to attain.

"Debris," 1

Prajna is the dynamic aspect of Suchness.

The crucial mystery: the "me" is unreal, yet Reality is immanent in, and and transcendent to, all manifestation.

When one gains an insight into the reality "behind" manifestation one should perceive the reality "behind" the "me"— one's own and other people's personalities. At the same moment the unreality of the apparent "me" becomes evident: it is a distorted reflection of the moon in a puddle.

Is one not *everyone* in one's dreams? And when one is awake (as it is called)?

All concepts are dualistic, therefore in order to transcend dualism (the opposites and complementaries) we must transcend concepts. That is known as direct cognition.

Not worth writing down? Perhaps.

A concept is an arrestation of the movement of manifestation; so it is *ipso facto* a dead thing, without reality. So every concept is dead and unreal. To be seized, Reality must be approached before the formation of a concept, and in movement.

Suffering is exclusive to the false "me." It is therefore self-imposed. What we think is its cause is merely some phenomenon that releases the machinery of self-torture.

As Jehan Dufresne de Gallier said to me: "The fictitious 'me' of men who have understood is like a 'ham' actor who by force of habit goes on playing a part to an empty 'house.'"

It is also like a conjuror who performs his tricks in front of an audience that knows how they are done.

The fictitious "me" of men who have understood is a clown who has lost his "public." Poor devil!

Is birth a beginning rather than an end? Is death an end rather than a beginning?

Appearance as Reflection of Reality

Unreality is every object that we perceive sensorially. Nothing that we perceive can be real, nor any attribute that we may give it. Reality is the thing-in-itself, in its Thusness or Suchness.

What we perceive is something projected by our psycho-somatic apparatus, within ourselves, for nothing apparent exists outside our mind; the immanent or subjacent reality we can know only by intuition or direct cognition. But how may we comprehend that immanent Thusness?

Objects sensorially perceived, so regarded, may be conceived as reflections of real vision, revealing external aspects only (form and colour) in three dimensions instead of the within (the essence) in four.

But in real vision there is no longer duality: vision and witness of vision are one and identical. Time, being, as we have seen, the tridimensional manner in which the fourth dimension of Space is perceived, disappears automatically and inevitably in quadridimensional vision, and with it the dualism of seer and seen in no-longer-existent Space-time (for seeing and seen imply both Space and Time).

Further, the figure, or even the object, with which we identify ourselves in our dreams is no more nor less ourselves than any other component of such dream, but is merely an element therein. Awake (as we call it) the situation is doubtless the same; i.e. we are neither more nor less ourselves than we are in any other element within the compass of our minds.

The Witness of perception is all equally, and alone is real.

The act of perceiving (sensorially) is real; that which is perceived is unreal.

This brief statement is more important than it appears.

The act of every action is real, the action (in its effect) is unreal. This is surely the meaning of the Zen Masters' technique of blows, kicks, gestures, exclamations.

In applied Zen, in archery, in swordsmanship, etc., the technique amounts to a discarding of reasoned actions and the substitution of spontaneous ones, an abandonment of the unreal processes of thought thereby leaving the way open for the real to act directly. Inevitably when that is allowed to happen the time-factor is by-passed and action and reaction become simultaneous. Consequently, without aim (reasoning) and with relaxed muscles, one arrow splits its predecessor in the bull's-eye, and the parry accompanies the thrust—so that the technically efficient (reasoning) swordsman, however swift his reflexes, faces inevitable death or defeat.

But is not this the doctrine of Lao Tzu and Chuang Tzu, the application of the Taoist *Wu-Wei?*

To use the title Zen Buddhism and never Zen Taoism is surely an historical anomaly.

The Relationship between Reality and Manifestation

My understanding of manifestation or the world of appearances or the ten thousand things is that we perceive, and can only perceive, sensorially, what in our terminology has to be described as the external aspect of reality (although Reality cannot have either outside or inside). That aspect is merely that which perception in three-dimensions-plus-time is able to seize and interpret. Dimensions, however, are only a laboratory apparatus devised for the purpose of analysis and comprehension, and do not exist as things-in-themselves.

It has been demonstrated that the higher animals, though living in what to us is a three-dimensional world, have percepts only and a two-dimensional consciousness, although tridimensional consciousness and vague concepts may occasionally be achieved. If that is so the analogy with ourselves seems to be perfect. We who live in a four-dimensional world have percepts and concepts and a three-dimensional consciousness, although quadridimensional consciousness and intuitional cognition may occasionally supervene. Each category has the higher as a potentiality.

Since Time is known to be the fourth dimension of Space and at the same time a function of our receptive apparatus it automatically disappears on the attainment of quadridimensional perception wherein things are no longer perceived in succession. Moreover, since in tridimensional vision only the external aspect of objects can ever be perceived, so in quadridimensional vision must the further dimension of objects become visible—which is that which to us is "within." But this "within" may merely be that which we normally perceive in succession as externals. Furthermore, motion being a function of time, and so unreal, disappears also in real vision, for non-action is a function of Reality (or of Tao, as the great Sage termed it).

That which is then perceived, in real vision as it is called, is the thusness or suchness of things, the self-nature of things, that which the Zen Masters perceived and sought to render visible to their disciples by forcibly drawing their attention, away from reasoning which is unreal, to things-in-themselves by means of the *act* of action and of perception which is the only element of reality therein.

But these things perceived are not objects external to ourselves: from a mirage to a mountain their only degree of existence, a relative one, is in our own mind. All duality is unreal, is merely the mode of conception available to us, unicity of vision being divided into perceiver and perceived, into all the unreal opposites and complementaries, for the purpose of interpretation in concepts. In real vision duality must also disappear and the unity of perceiver and perceived be re-established. But that is the vision of the Buddha, the vision of Reality itself, and it would appear likely, to me at any rate, that such vision represented a further stage of cognition than that attained by the satori of the Zen Masters, an increase of perception involving the transcendence of more than four of our dimensional limitations.

To sum up, Reality is the Tao, the Absolute, other than which nothing is, immobile, timeless, spaceless—such attributes being merely imaginary values used by us as a means of arriving at some kind of understanding of what Reality must be but having no validity whatsoever as things-in-themselves. But Reality, being everything, is necessarily immanent, transcendent, subjacent, infused in everything that we can know, think, or imagine, however far from Reality itself such percepts and concepts may be in their duality. Thus everything from a mirage to a mountain is unreal, yet everything from a mirage to a mountain must be a reflection of Reality.

Ed. note: See *The Zen Teaching of Hui Hai* by John Blofeld, Rider and Co., 1962.

19 ·– Time and Space - VI

"Debris," 2

Time is the key to the metaphysical problem.

When we come to understand the function of Time the principle problems will be seen no longer to exist.

Time, I have quoted from Kant, is a function of our receptive apparatus. But are not all our perceptions dependent on Time (as the fourth dimension of Space)? Therefore . . .

Motion, being a function of Time, is therefore a function of our receptive apparatus, and unreal. Non-action, immobility, in its ultimate character of Non-Action, is a function of Tao or Reality.

According to the oriental approach it is said that without Cause-and-Effect Time and Space are inconceivable. That in itself seems to be placing Effect before Cause. For indeed without Time and Space Cause-and-Effect are inconceivable. Cause-and-Effect *only* exist as a function of Time and Space (as Time and Space exist as a function of our psychosomatic apparatus). There seems little indication that Time was understood in the East.

What is called *Maya* is that which results from the concepts called Time and Space.

Looked at in another manner *Maya* may be said to be the limitation of tridimensional consciousness represented by Space, Time, and Causality.

"If a person wishes to make a study of illusion, in spite of the fact that his own body is an illusion, we are reduced to the absurdity of an illusion studying an illusion." (Chang Chan).

Definition of a classical psychoanalyst: an illusion treating a sick illusion for an illusionary sickness.

20 ·~ Work and Play - IV

Men and Women, 1

The evolution of man seems to call for intimate association with a variety of women, with each of whom the required interaction takes place, from each of whom he obtains, and to each of whom he gives, something essential to development.

The evolution of woman is no different but is obstructed by the urge for possession which drives her to any lengths in the phantasmagoric attempt to acquire exclusive possession of one man for all time. But what is there *there* to possess? It is hardly possible to possess the unsubstantial, a puff of smoke, an echo, the reflection of the moon in a puddle, and even handcuffs do not constitute possession—as a poet explained in famous lines referring to prison walls.

The permanent association of one man and one woman, though it may conceivably have some social utility, appears to be a hindrance to the adequate utilisation of a life, and so to full temporal realisation. Are we not obliged to suppose that the plenitude of intemporal realisation depends on the degree of temporal realisation that precedes it?

The urge for possession is an example of the familiar

process of identification by the ego, and should effectively impede any approach to the perception of Reality.

It has been said that no human being can possess another. Every human life is essentially lonely; an old bachelor is no more lonely than a young one; a bachelor than a man with a wife whom he dislikes; a man with a wife whom he dislikes than one with a wife whom he loves; a man with a wife than a man with a harem.

Reality, being both immanent and transcendent, may be said to be *infused* in all manifestation. One may suspect that it may be immanent rather than transcendent in the more subtle relations between man and woman.

Rights and Possessions

On the material plane we have certain "rights" according to certain laws, which on that plane we can exercise. We can "possess" by law a house, a garden, a motor-car, and even a wife, and on the same plane we can dispossess ourselves of such articles and such "rights."

But in fact we have never possessed anything, and we never could. If it comes to that—what is there to possess? And who is there to possess anything or nothing?

21 ·- Reality and Manifestation - VII

The act of perception itself is probably non-dualistic; it is memory ("habit-energy") that creates duality.

Perceptions have become memory by the time we seize them; it is the memory only that we know—and that is presented relatively (by a comparison of the opposites).

If non-dual perceptions were seized they would at the same time be non-egoistic.

⤫

"In reality there are no living beings to be liberated by the Tathagata." (The Buddha in the Diamond Sutra, XXV)

Why? Because the process of "living" (in "time" and "space") is an illusion. *We* are not an illusion in so far as we ARE, but our living on the plane of existence (or seeming) is illusory.

22 ·- The Ego - I

Between Ourselves

PERSONA (literally "mask": the artificial "me"): You say that I don't exist, that I have no reality; you liken me to a puff of smoke, vapour, a passing cloud, even a mirage. But here I am.

RELATIVE EGO: Look, there is a passing cloud!

PERSONA: Then what am I?

RELATIVE EGO: You are the resultant of all my contacts with the "not-me." Your substance is memory, also called "habit energy," your vitality is psychic tension, and you live on affirmations and negations.

PERSONA: Is my substance not real?

RELATIVE EGO: Memory is not real; it is like a reflection or echo of that which has been perceived and is no longer perceived—though it has not ceased to be; it is a distorted image of a perception.

PERSONA: Even if I am not real, how can you maintain that I do not exist?

RELATIVE EGO: Because you are not a thing-in-itself. You only exist in the colloquial sense that everything we recognise may be said therefore to have an appearance of existence. You are an evaluation, not a reality.

PERSONA: Yet you and your friends spend a lot of time talking about me as though I existed. You say that the ego of so-and-so sticks out like the bristles on a hedgehog, that such another has an ego like a boil on his nose, that a third is an "insufferable egoist." You have just been saying that pride and humility are merely functions of the ego, that when I am powerful they manifest as pride, and that when I am weak they manifest as humility. How can they be a function of something that does not exist?

RELATIVE EGO: They do not exist as things-in-themselves just as you do not, and for precisely the same reason; just as they are merely estimations of a function depending on you, so you are also just a functional manifestation.

PERSONA: So they are a function of a function? What is a function?

RELATIVE EGO: It is defined as "a quantity that is dependent for its value on another quantity." No function exists as a thing-in-itself.

PERSONA: Of what am I a function?

RELATIVE EGO: Of me.

PERSONA: And what, pray, are you?

RELATIVE EGO: As Bodhidharma stated long ago to the Emperor of China in reply to the same question—I do not know.

PERSONA: Is that a qualification for accusing others of not existing?

RELATIVE EGO: I am a function of maya. When Reality refracts Itself through the prism of Time, and appears in Mind as manifestation in three dimensions—which is maya—I appear as the nucleus of this so-called individual.

PERSONA: Why so-called?

RELATIVE EGO: Because the word "individual" means that which is undivided, and the manifestation in question is just the opposite of that. He is a "dividual," but he has the superficial appearance of singularity.

PERSONA: Multiple or single, are you real at least?

RELATIVE EGO: Good Heavens, no: I am relative.

PERSONA: That is a comfort.

RELATIVE EGO: Thinking of yourself as usual!

PERSONA: That is my job. How do you know that you are not real?

RELATIVE EGO: The Lord Buddha, in the Diamond Sutra, many times used a phrase which was admirably inclusive. That which must not be conceived as really existing he termed "an ego-entity, a personality, a being or a separated individuality." We are all in that.

PERSONA: Well, what is the difference between us?

RELATIVE EGO: I fulfill a useful function; without me this so-called individual would disintegrate, could not remain in manifestation.

PERSONA: And me?

RELATIVE EGO: You are just a nuisance, a by-product, a malady, a bad smell. I have only to cut off the psychic tensions which are your life-force, or deprive you of the affirmations and negations on which you feed, and you dissolve like a puff of smoke, vapour, or a cloud in the sky.

PERSONA: You try! I am strong; I know how to fight and protect myself.

RELATIVE EGO: Nonsense, you are a clown, an illusionist. When one grows up and sees through the tawdry mechanism of your tricks, and watches you performing them, you wilt and crumple up like a balloon that is burst. Your strength is that of a bully, but you are only a poor fish. You have nothing substantial anywhere in you to hold you together. You are just hot air.

PERSONA: You think you are somebody just because you have Reality behind you, attached to your name by a hyphen.

RELATIVE EGO: Potentially I am Reality, but as long as I am encumbered with you I am tied down to perception in three dimensions and can only know that intellectually. When I am rid of you I shall be free to turn round—paravritti it is called in Sanscrit, the "turning over of the mind"—and live in accordance with cosmic necessity, free from conflict, free from all the miseries that come upon me through your antics. I shall be able to cast off relativity.

PERSONA: Can't I come in on that?

RELATIVE EGO: In that state there remains no sense of a "me," there is no longer differentiation between one and other. How then could you participate therein?

PERSONA: That's all ballyhoo; I'm off to see if I can't find a means of having a good time. I "exist" all right in my own way.

RELATIVE EGO: Incorrigible! What a lout! You could not understand it, but to "exist" connotes "dualistically"; all idea of existence is dualistic. That is why it is unreal, why nothing exists in reality—as Hui Neng told us. But "being" is always in unicity. And nothing dualist (relative) IS.

23 ·– *Physics and Metaphysics - V*

Satori—Does It Exist?

On the plane of being everything IS. On the plane of existing everything seems.

There are no living beings (as the Lord Buddha said) because living is a function of Time and exists only on the plane of seeming.

Being IS (even our language makes that conclusion inevitable), but "living beings"—beings apparently engaged in the process of changing from hour to hour, year to year— are a function of Time and merely (seem to) exist.

Enlightenment IS: it is just the normal state of being (as opposed to existing). Thus it was possible for the Lord Buddha to say that no such thing as "Enlightenment" exists either—for if it is the state of being it has no need of a name, is nothing separate and nameable, and can only be so called as an estimation regarded from the plane of seeming.

It is clear therefore why the Masters said there was nothing to be attained, that "there are no such states as before and after attainment," for you cannot attain something you already have, and there can be no states of before and after something that is already there.

But, looked at from the plane of seeming, there "seems" to be something to be attained, and states of before and after such attainment, and that something is the turning over of the mind—*paravritti*, liberation, enlightenment, sambodhi, satori—but so to regard it would be deliberately to adopt the false vision of the plane of seeming (or dualism) which it was the aim of the Masters to eradicate.

Applied Zen and Real Zen

Zen that can be taught cannot be real Zen.

Anything obtained by discipline, anything that can be learned, must *ipso facto* be a fake. Knowledge being intuitive, reasoning or training can only produce a substitute or an imitation.

Zen is not communicable in words: it can only be suggested or pointed at.

Zazen and meditation are disciplines and in the nature of substitutes for satori. As such they should be a barrier to the realisation of what they seek to reveal.

They may lead to the experience known as *ken-sho*—but has not that been found to be just that—a barrier to permanent enlightenment?

Meditation and "quiet-sitting" have been roundly condemned by some of the greatest Masters.

Zeal was condemned two thousand years before Talleyrand said quietly to an official: "Et . . . surtout pas de zèle!"

The quoted definitions of Huang Po and Hui Hai prove that Dhyana, Ch'an, Zen means Non-attachment, and that Non-attachment means the absence of feelings such as hatred and love. Therefore the use of the word "meditation" as a translation is quite misleading (see *What is Zen? 1* and *What is Zen? 3*).

However, a state of pellucid-attention-devoid-of-ideation is in accordance with Zen and may also be considered as a form of meditation—thus completing the circle and reconciling the two concepts.

❧

The Lord Buddha himself, and many Masters after him, stated that there was nothing to be attained and that there are no such states as before and after attainment. This has just been explained in detail.

As long as there remains identification with an imaginary ego the state we describe (from the plane of seeming) as Enlightenment cannot be experienced, but as soon as such identification ceases and dualism can be transcended *that state alone remains*. For that state alone IS.

Intellectual comprehension is not capable of dispelling this illusory identification—for an eye cannot see itself. Only intuitive comprehension should be capable of producing that apparent turning over of the mind (*paravritti*) which is realisation. Such a turning-over may be just a turning of our gaze from time to beyond it, from without to within.

Jesus said, "The Kingdom of Heaven is within." "Within" is our notion of the invisible dimension. It may be enough to look in the right direction.

What could there be to teach? What result could any

technique or discipline be expected to produce that was not a fake?

What is there to do but let our gaze follow the pointing fingers of the Masters? When comprehension follows, the illusion should be dissipated.

Call that satori if you will, or enlightenment, but such words are evaluations of the false vision from the plane of seeming. There is nothing but seeing what is already there.

Wasps

Are we not wasps who spend all day in a fruitless attempt to traverse a window-pane—while the other half of the window is wide open?

Were not the Zen Masters eternally pointing with their finger to the open window, a gesture which we wasps do not seem able to follow?

Wasps seem to lack the sense of one dimension. And we?

Live Thought or Dead? The Zen Point of View

Ce qui peut etre exprimé ne peut etre vrai.
—OUSPENSKY

The Masters of Zen rarely discoursed. Discoursing they regarded as one of the obstacles to enlightenment, for it encouraged and developed the wrong kind of thinking—that "mentation" or "intellection" which affirms our false identification with a fictitious ego.

"The ignorant are delighted with discoursing," the Lankavatara Sutra states, "discoursing is a source of suffering in the triple world." We would not doubt it; yes, indeed, but when the Lanka says that discoursing is a source of suffering it means more particularly that it is a hindrance to the removal of ignorance, and so perpetuates our normal state of suffering.

But, nowadays, what was meant by discoursing is chiefly represented by books. In books, as conventionally and commercially produced today, no idea can be conveyed in less than about ten thousand words—with apologies for not making it a hundred thousand, in which form it would have been much "better." No chance for anyone to think except the author!

Yet, when ideas are buried in a haystack of verbiage, who remembers them, and, conversely, when ideas are concisely expressed, who pays any attention to them? The most vital statements of the sages and prophets, even of the Buddha and Jesus, are not taken seriously—presumably because they are not served up in a sauce that conceals their flavour and substitutes its own.

Instead of apologising for not burying their ideas even more deeply in verbiage would not modern authors do better to apologise whenever they are unable to express an idea more concisely than in, say, one thousand words? Ideas may vary in the amount of expression they need; for many a hundred words should be ample. After all, the more fully expressed the less juice there remains in them, the more complete the exposition the more dead they are on delivery; ideas mummified in words are only museum specimens.

The ideas of the Masters, expressed in half a dozen words, are still alive after centuries, but they are fingers pointing to intuitional understanding, not fossilised examples of intellection.

24 ⁓ Reality and Manifestation – VIII

Discrimination and Discrimination

One of the essential teachings of the Masters to which we in the West most consistently close our eyes is their repeated condemnation of "mentation," "intellection," which connotes wrong thinking, the wrong kind of thinking, mental activity which affirms our identification with an imaginary ego and so hinders the elimination of what is called "ignorance," and renders liberation therefrom and living in a state of enlightenment forever impossible.

The above is an omnibus statement. It should suffice to say that wrong thinking is mental activity on the plane of seeming. Do we understand this? What do we do about it? Have we any reason to doubt that the Masters knew what they were saying and meant what they said? If we are serious we should act upon their advice. If we do not—what result can we ever expect to obtain?

Also we are apt to be appalled when we find "discrimination" roundly condemned, as all the Masters condemn it, and then, on the next page, "discrimination" lauded as a high and essential activity of the bodhisattva. The explanation is simple enough once it is understood. Discrimination on the plane of seeming is equivalent to identification and attachment, for it is affective; but discrimination on the plane of intuitive cognition is neither more nor less than vision of Reality.

The incalculable value of the brief statements of Hsi Yun and Hui Hai lies in that they, and they alone, explain these things to us.

As regards discrimination on the plane of seeming no quotation is necessary, since every Master has condemned it, and an explanation is offered above. As regards correct discrimination Hui Hai says this:

"An equal combination of abstraction ('abstraction' here means detachment from affectivity) and understanding is called deliverance."

"To be able to distinguish minutely between every kind of good and evil is called understanding. Not to feel love or hatred or to be in any way affected at the moment of making these distinctions is called abstraction (detachment). This is an equal combination of abstraction (detachment) and understanding."

And, therefore, "is called *deliverance.*"

But let us not forget that on the plane of seeming discrimination, that is affective discrimination, between "good" and "evil" is illusory.

Hui Hai also states, "No attachment means that feelings of hatred and love do not arise. That is what is meant by no attachment."

The Void: What Is It?

Have we a greater difficulty than the famous "Void" which forms the principal subject of so many sutras and statements of the Masters as of the Buddha himself? How many hair-splitting definitions, negations of negations and contradictions of contradictions have been attempted in order to suggest its meaning to our tridimensional minds?

Supposing we ask Hui Hai?

"The Void is simply non-attachment" (Section 25). Did that not need saying? Does it not say enough?*

It may be necessary to regard the Void in a more metaphysical aspect. "Emptiness," "the Void"—if one thinks about it, surely the epithet most suggestive and least misleading to us today should be just "Non-Manifestation"?

If anything is clear it is that the Taoist conception of Non-Action is the basis of all action. Similarly Non-manifestation must be the basis of all manifestation.

Huang Po regards phenomenal or sensory experience as universal mind wrongly apprehended, form and real nature being therefore identical (Section 5).

Let me put it like this: Manifestation and Non-Manifestation are identical, but we have an inaccurate (because tridimensional) perception of Reality which we call phenomena.

This inaccurate perception may be presumed to be neither more nor less than the limitative faculty of perceiving the fourth dimension of space serially in what we know as Time.

This conception of Huang Po should perhaps be regarded as fundamental in Zen after Hui Neng, and is to be retained.

---

* *Ed. note:* See John Blofeld's *The Zen Teaching of Hui Hai* and *The Zen Teaching of Huang Po.*

Most, if not all, sects of most, if not all, superior religions seek to transmute hate into love, that is negative into positive. Zen alone requires no such transmutation, between two aspects of a single thing, which are evaluations of an affective manifestation. Instead it requires absolute non-attachment, the exclusion of both hate and love, which may be defined as the abolition of affectivity itself. One may look for the origin of this in the original Taoism.

But if *Caritas*, impersonal compassion, be an accurate description of the resulting state, one must envisage it as a strictly non-affective condition of the mind.

Evolution of the Ego

May we not conveniently regard the persona (mask), or false "me," as a function of the relative ego, wherein lies its particular unreality?

When the relative "me" begins to understand and evolve, the false "me," which depends upon it, is modified and sub-sides in ratio to such evolution. If enlightenment is realised the false "me" is thereby cut off from its source and extin-guished—for the relative "me" has abandoned its relativity.

25 ⸱⟶ *Physics and Metaphysics - VI*

Dimensions of the Mind, 1

Are not Percepts a function of consciousness in two dimensions,

Concepts a function of consciousness in three dimensions,

Intuitive Cognitions a function of consciousness in four dimensions?

❧

Attachment, being clearly dependent on material objects, percepts and concepts, is evidently a tridimensional phenomenon.

Equally evidently "Non-Attachment" appertains to the further dimension. It is intuitive and—so it would seem—leads directly to the goal.

❧

Dimensions do not belong to external objects: they are a property of the mind. An external object has as many dimensions as the mind attributes to it.

❧

Just as a line is the limit of a two-dimensional plane, so is a two-dimensional plane (a surface) the limit of a cube, and a three-dimensional object must necessarily be the limit (all that can be seen) of a four-dimensional object.

As tridimensional beings everything we see is the limit or exterior of the hyper-dimensional "reality."

❧

Perhaps it is we, passing a quadridimensional field, who thereby see the fourth dimension in movement as Time, just as an animal, moving on a plane surface such as a road, sees a house which he passes as "turning," the tree as "moving forward" into his path as he approaches.

26 ·- *Time and Space - VII*

The T-Bomb

The number of our conceptions which depend upon the
Time-illusion is considerable—and all must necessarily be
nonsense. Our notions of birth, death, life itself, survival,
rebirth—all are inevitably utter rubbish! And how many
more, on which we base our way of "living," on which we
have built our psychical edifice? Realise this, i.e. take away
the Time-illusion, and what is left?
A resounding and ubiquitous crash!
In fact, has anyone yet dared to do it?
Attaboy!

The Eternal Present

In Time the Present does not exist, that is it has no recognisable duration and almost certainly no duration of any kind
whatever. It separates the "Past" from the "Future" in the
same theoretical manner as that in which the equator separates the Northern Hemisphere from the Southern, i.e. symbolically. That is, of course, regarded tridimensionally, on the
plane of existence or seeming.
Quadridimensionally regarded, the Present eternally IS, for
Past and Future are not, or, if you prefer, they are Present, but
it has no quality of time, that is no kind of duration or continuity (succession).

Prophecy

Prophecy, in so far as it exists, can only be vision into a

dimension beyond the time-barrier. But the seer does not behold the future, what is to come, but the present, and what is.

One of the greatest difficulties experienced by prophets has always been in placing what they have seen into our illusory time-sequence. What they see may be past or future to us, and how can they tell? They have to guess. Usually I think they are mistaken. It was probably the Trojan War, and they mistook Ulysses for the Kaiser, and Menelaos for Mussolini.

27 ⸺ *Physics and Metaphysics – VII*

Dimensions of the Mind, 2

Confusion arises from the tendency, due to our life-long conditioning, to regard dimensions as appertaining to the external world, whereas there can only be dimensions of mind. It is in us, not in what we perceive, that dimensionality functions.

The men of mathematical and scientific discipline who first thought of studying the possibility of hyperdimensions inevitably regarded them as appertaining to phenomena (which to them were reality). That, no doubt, is why their investigations remained theoretical.

For us no such error should be possible, though it was less an error than a faulty approach to the problem, for we have been told that Mind itself is Reality, and that nothing can exist outside it.

If we care to consider consciousness as having four states or degrees, stretching from the lowest form of life to the highest, and if we choose to equate each with a dimension— remembering that a dimension is nothing magical or even

complicated but merely means a direction of measurement—
we arrive at a table of equivalents that has a nice air of
verisimilitude:

1st state of consciousness — instinctive, or D.1
2nd state of consciousness — perceptive, or D.2
3rd state of consciousness — conceptual, or D.3
4th state of consciousness — intuitive, or D.4

Let us take this analysis still further in the hope of seeing
more clearly.

We may attribute to Mind Itself (universal, cosmic Mind)
a state of extra-dimensionality, comprising all possible
dimensions, like the Plenitude of the Void. That is Non-
Manifestation. But Mind-in-manifestation can be given categories for our convenience, based on the degree of evolution
of consciousness, from that which we attribute to the plant,
via that which we attribute to animals, to that which we
attribute to ourselves. To each of these categories a measurement of the evolution of consciousness may tentatively be
applied, and each such measurement, apart from degrees of
development within the category, may imply what is called a
dimension. And, corresponding to each such dimension there
may be a fuller mode of comprehension as suggested in the
above table.

The tridimensional consciousness not only has percepts, as
the animal has, but also concepts, and the result of such concepts is the objective world as we see it.

But the quadridimensional consciousness acquires knowledge directly, by what we term intuition, and we all have that
faculty as a potentiality. The enlightened human being has
realised that potentiality and lives in that higher state of consciousness which we regard as having four dimensions.

The Sages and Prophets who have taught mankind from
that state of consciousness, including the founders of the

great religions, make it clear that this potential consciousness is available to all of us, is indeed our natural state and our heritage. And we have only to look in the right direction, and open our eyes, in order to enjoy it. But the right direction is at right-angles to all others (for every dimension by definition is that)—and that is what we call "within"; we cannot open our eyes as long as they are clouded by false notions, or look in the right direction as long as our attention is fixed on a fictitious ego apparently "without."

Real religion may be recognised as approximately this, and not the disciplinary application of an artificial system of ethics, for the recorded words of their founders point to it.

"Dimension," then, is just a technical term we use to indicate states of consciousness increasing in scope, from one to four, of Mind-in-manifestation. The phenomena of which we become conscious by these means increase in scope as each potential dimension is realised, for they are Reality imperfectly apprehended.

But we too are phenomena, and we too are Reality imperfectly apprehended; and Reality and Mind Itself are one and all that IS.

The fulfilment of this potentiality, called enlightenment, satori, etc., is said to be the realisation of this. As long as it remains a potentiality we can know it conceptually (that is know *about* it) only; to know it (by intuitive cognition) is realisation of the quadridimensional state of consciousness.

I have said that the fictitious ego is apparently "without." But to us, on the plane of phenomena, it seems to be "within." We are mistaken, however, and the mistake is crucial. Reality alone is "within."

28 ·- *Reality and Manifestation - IX*

The personality that results from all the contacts of the individual with his environment between conception and death, that which we have called the false "me," the artificial ego, the persona, is necessarily the product of tridimensional consciousness—percepts and concepts. Being a tridimensional product such personality cannot but partake of the unreality and impermanence of all that belongs to that plane of seeming.

Obvious? Of course.

"You cannot use mind to seek something from mind."

"Mind and the object of its search are one." (Huang Po)

But these apparently unimpressive statements are probably of the utmost possible significance.

Long Fingers

Ramana Maharshi, our contemporary widely known in the West, and universally admitted a man of satori or enlightenment, allowed the Swami Nityabodhananda to question him on this subject.

In reply to one query he answered, "You asked me if any difference exists between the 'normal' state of ordinary people and that of men who are 'realised.' What have they *real*-ised? Only that which is real in themselves. But that which is real in them is equally real in you. Wherein lies a difference?"

That which is *not* real is clearly the artificial ego and everything pertaining to it, indeed everything tridimensional in the psyche. Following the Maharshi's pointing finger do we not find ourselves looking at the quadridimensional mind? If so, let us glance once more at the pointing fingers of Huang Po, cited above, and follow the direction in which they lead our gaze. Is that not at right-angles to the three visible dimensions? Is that not Within? (wherein lies the "kingdom of Heaven," according to Jesus.)

❧

The Maharshi also reiterated to the Swami what he had already declared to Professor Sarma, that at no time in his life had he practised any kind of *sadhana* (spiritual discipline) "worthy of the name," nor was any such practice necessary.

He added later, "How could you doubt the reality of this 'I' which is questioning? This 'I' is your 'normal' state. What effort, then, would you have to make in order to enter into this normal state?"

He also said, "That which you take to be your normal state is, on the contrary, an abnormal state. . . . Do you have to search for a long time before finding this 'I' that is none other than yourself? That is what I mean when I declare that no spiritual discipline (*sadhana*) is necessary in order to realise the Self. All one asks of you is that you abstain from doing anything whatever (of a disciplinary nature), that you remain calm, and finally that you be *that which you really are.* You have only to free yourself from the hypnotic spell in which your abnormal state holds you."

The "Self" in question—in case one should forget—is impersonal. It is also what the Zen Masters and the sutras called "the self-nature," "the original face," "the Buddha nature."

Let us remember that this comes from a man of our own times, living in a state of enlightenment. It is, as we say, "straight from the horse's mouth." And how perfectly it accords with what Huang Po and Hui Hai told us, also in plain straightforward words, a thousand years ago!

29 · Physics and Metaphysics - VIII

Normal and Abnormal

Inevitably mind functions in a fourth dimension—for it is neither in front nor behind, at one side or the other, above or below, but "within" or in depth.

Mind *itself* functions in a fourth dimension of measurement ("dimension")—that is beyond contestation—but our psycho-somatic apparatus confines its manifestation to the three in which are revealed by our senses what we know as phenomena.

Therefore tridimensionality appears to reside in our psycho-somatic apparatus, and what we experience as consciousness has been adapted by that. But mind itself knows no such limitation. That is why our "normal" state is that of mind, and our "abnormal" state that in which our senses confine us.

Detachment

What, after all, is it—regarded in our practical occidental manner of thinking? Is it not just this, that it is necessary to detach oneself from the limitations of habits, imposed by our three-dimensional conditioning, in order freely to make use of the fourth?

We must leave D.3 in order to enter D.4.

❧

Detachment is a state, it is not a totalisation of achieved indifferences.

A Dialogue, 1

TWO: "You cannot use mind to seek something from mind." What is sought from mind?

ONE: Reality.

TWO: And what is the mind we might seek to use in the search?

ONE: Reality.

TWO: But our limited consciousness in three dimensions?

ONE: "An inaccurate apprehension of Reality."

TWO: Can we not use that?

ONE: How could it be effective?

TWO: So what does Hsi Yun mean?

ONE: That there is nothing to seek, and no means of seeking it. For it is already there, and it is all that there is anywhere at all. I know of nothing else that he could mean.

TWO: So what do we do?

ONE: Nothing need be done or can be done, for there is nothing to do and nothing with which to do anything.

TWO: But I seek realisation.

ONE: It is there. You have it. Look—instead of thinking about looking. Reality is in the act of looking, not in what your tridimensional consciousness thinks it has seen.

TWO: Go on.

ONE: It is the Goose in the Bottle again. The answer, as

you know, is, "Look, it is out!"

A Dialogue, 2

TWO: "Mind and the object of its search are one." What is the object of its search?

ONE: Reality.

TWO: Therefore the mind itself is Reality?

ONE: The Mind itself is Reality, but our vision of it is a concept, and therefore tridimensional, and that is "an inaccurate apprehension of Reality."

TWO: So the object of our search is just Mind, and we have it already.

ONE: That would seem to be so.

TWO: But what have we to do in order to see it as it really is?

ONE: Just open our eyes, and look.

TWO: But all we see is a concept?

ONE: Alas!

TWO: What then?

ONE: The act of every action is real, the percept of every perception is real, reality is basic in everything we can do or experience. Essentially everything is real. We live in reality. We are real. All we need is to real-ise it.

TWO: And yet in everyday experience all this reality is "inaccurately apprehended." How can we come to apprehend it accurately?

ONE: As long as we remain identified with a tridimensional self, based on memories of our past experiences on the plane of seeming, a temporary and artificial structure, as anyone can see, it does not appear to be possible for us to apprehend it accurately.

TWO: How may we free ourselves from this identification?

ONE: The method is called non-attachment (or Dhyana or Zen).

TWO: How is that to be applied?

ONE: By not reacting with hatred or love to that which we perceive, by not judging affectively, by not making affective estimations and evaluations of everything that enters our consciousness.

TWO: In short, by not reacting affectively?

ONE: And by dispassionately watching the antics of our pseudo-self. That is my understanding of the teaching of those who were living in a state of enlightenment when they taught.

TWO: But what effect can that have?

ONE: We have just succeeded in creating a concept which represents an intellectual apprehension of Reality, but it is only a concept in tridimensional consciousness. That may seem to be something achieved, but actually it is nothing. We are exactly where we were before we made it. Before it can function it must be transmuted into real knowledge, prajna, or quadridimensional realisation.

TWO: I know that, but how?

ONE: No one has ever described the mechanism, probably because there is none. I think we only have to look—in the right direction.

TWO: Which is?

ONE: All dimensions are, by definition, at right-angles to all others.

TWO: In this case—Within?

ONE: Inevitably.

TWO: And we shall see?

ONE: Inevitably.

TWO: Once and for all?

ONE: Inevitably.

TWO: And what is hindering us from so-doing now?

ONE: Nothing. That is, nothing real: just attachment, attachment which prevents us from looking in the right direction. But that attachment is an illusory thing—like the chalk line which prevents the chicken from taking its beak off the ground.

TWO: And that is all?

ONE: That is my understanding of the teaching of the Masters. If you have another it should be as worthy of consideration as mine.

Percepts, Concepts, and Direct Cognition

If we analyse a percept what do we observe? A sense-impression in *not more than two dimensions at a time*. If we analyse a concept what do we observe? Percepts in not more than two dimensions associated by a further process of the mind so that they are comprehended as three-dimensional objects.

The concept of a cube, a table, a house, is an *interpretation* of perceptions of surfaces and colours.

The concept is due to the power of synthesis and interpretation, which that animal lacks; this seems to demonstrate the accuracy of our supposition whereby the two-dimensional consciousness is confined to percepts, which the three-dimensional consciousness translates into concepts.

The four-dimensional power of direct cognition is difficult for us to analyse who do not have it as a regular faculty, but it would seem to transcend form (percepts and concepts) and not to be subject to space and time as conceived tridimensionally. That was to be expected; one might say that so it must be by definition. Since it short-circuits the tridimensional reasoning faculty it cannot be expected to conform to our rules of logic.

Since it is knowledge of a wider nature, arrived at by a fuller mode, it cannot readily be expressed in language designed to describe knowledge that is limited to a dimension less. Crystallised in words or image, necessarily of a dimension less than its own, it is more likely to appear to be nonsense than sense.

The Goose and Its Apparent Bottle. It's Out!

The famous koan of the goose in the bottle, to be got out without harming the goose or breaking the bottle, has a very simple and obvious solution to our eyes—whatever may have been the intention of the Zen Masters who imagined it.

It should be as easy to extract a goose from a bottle, or a man from a prison, as for a tridimensional being to move out of a confined area on a two-dimensional plane-surface. He just steps "over" the apparent obstacle (which is only such to the two-dimensional being). It merely requires the utilisation of a further dimension. If historical cases are factual it has often been done. The mind can do it at any moment.

Famous conundrums—perpetual motion, the philosopher's stone, squaring the circle, are insoluble problems only to tridimensional logic. To a quadridimensional mind they should be as simple as taking the goose out of the bottle.

30 ·~ *Reality and Manifestation - X*

Logic and Superlogic

The terms "illusory" and "unreal" are traditionally applied to the artificial ego, and even to all phenomena, but it is questionable whether such terms may not be misleading to the literal mind of the modern man. Such words have only relative value here—for nothing can be absolutely unreal. Since only Reality IS, whatever exists—though it BE not—must partake of Reality. Phenomena, as has been said, are reality inaccurately apprehended—a choice expression of the translator of Huang Po.

I do not often make positive statements here, though it may not be possible or convenient to convey the tentative character of every statement made, but I am disposed to make one now:

There is no difference between Reality and Unreality, between the real and the unreal.

The apparent difference is a factor in our tridimensional apprehension. As such it exists on the plane of seeming, but it is not in Reality.

It should be salutary to bear this in mind.

In this matter we touch upon the unviability of the logic of the tridimensional mind when transcending the limits of three dimensions.

According to our logic we can say, "He is friendly," or "He is unfriendly," but not both together. But the quadridimensional mind can say both together, using our language, without illogicality.

Mind Is Not Mind

The method of instruction of Huang Po for the benefit of P'ei Hsin was to lead almost every concept to that of Mind-only. Then, suddenly, he mentions almost casually, "In fact, however, mind is not really mind."

This was the method employed by the Buddha in the Diamond Sutra on many occasions. To the positive logically-conditioned mind of modern man this treatment is apt to appall; the reader is distressed and discouraged. Yet, later, the effect can become salutary and refreshing. The reiteration of "Universal Mind" as the only thing that is, can be increasingly distressing, because it may appear as having less and less verisimilitude with every reiteration. In such case the sudden rejection of the concept may come with a welcome sense of relief.

The explanation of the method is obvious enough. In order to teach anything a concept is necessary, but if the concept comes to be taken as something that is, as something concrete, the teaching itself is thereby nullified. Therefore the concept just created has to be immediately destroyed.

Terms like "The Void," "Pure Consciousness," are perhaps as unpalatable as "Universal Mind," and have the same disadvantage. That is why one may prefer "Non-Manifestation" on which the image-making imagination has little hold, and which seems to be in the nature of a bridge between tridimensional concepts and quadridimensional knowledge.

The contradictions (enunciation and refutation of conceptions) of the Sages are probably not essentially different from the illogicality of the koans and mondo of the later Masters.

It is inevitable, and perhaps necessary, that seekers struggle to find a logical answer to them, strive to find a means of according them, or of effecting a synthesis. They must pass by there.

When a seeker no longer looks for a logical explanation he probably has understood something—whether he be aware of the fact or not.

When he is actually shocked and offended by a logical solution, and dismisses it from his mind in disgust, he has probably understood a good deal.

When he intuitively apprehends the real meaning—then he has presumably arrived.

The first stage represents a realisation of the insufficiency of tridimensional intellection. The second stage represents a realisation of the existence and validity of quadridimensional knowledge. The third stage represents its apprehension.

Hard Words, 1

The Intrinsic Value of Manifestation. What foundation could there be for the general notion of Mankind that the life of a human being, or of a million human beings, has any importance?

From a practical (political, economic, aesthetic) point of view the world would surely be a more desirable habitat if a thousand million human beings were to be removed from manifestation; just as should be the case as a result of the removal of a thousand billion flies.

May one not assume that the life or death of any living thing, in so far as it may be possible for us to judge, is a matter devoid of any kind of recognisable importance?

The notion that human life has any value *per se* is an unjustifiable assumption of human vanity.

The notion that human life has greater value than any other form of life is both unjustifiable and arrogant.

Hard Words, 2

De-bunking Time. Since phenomena depend upon Time, all human ideas that are based on phenomena necessarily depend on the time-factor, and must partake of the illusory character of that. One and all may be recognised as nonsense.

We talk of de-bunking this and that, but all our conceptions are necessarily bunk that do not discount time as a reality. The only de-bunking that has any meaning is one which disposes of every notion dependent on Time.

That which remains, if anything, might be the Truth.

The Myth of Forgiveness. There is no such thing as forgiveness on the plane of seeming. On the plane of reality there is nothing that requires forgiveness.

Psychologically regarded, on the phenomenal plane, no injury (real or imaginary) can ever be forgiven, no matter how keenly we may think we desire to forgive (though it may be counteracted by a service); on the noumenal plane no injury can be recognised as such.

The Eye That Cannot See Itself, 1

"Reality is too clamorous to be heard," as Jehan Dufresne de Gallier suggested. Yes, indeed; sounds, colours, flavours, all those sensations which are above or below the limited range of our senses, escape our apprehension.

But nothing is beyond the apprehension of our direct

cognition, of our *buddhi;* and Reality, for all that it seems to be nowhere, is nevertheless everywhere.

We have said it already: Reality is the act of every action, the percept of every perception, the being of each existence. We cannot perceive it, we cannot conceive it—but what prevents us from *knowing* it?

Reality is too clamorous to be heard; it is too ubiquitous to be seen; it cannot be taken hold of because we are it; but what is there to prevent one from realising that one IS?

Our identification with our mind, by any chance?

31 ·~ Work and Play - V

The Body

What is the truth about this body of ours that simple people mistake for themselves, with which all who are unenlightened identify themselves to some extent?

Take a film-star who owes (his or) her position less to talent than to the fact that great numbers of people regard her as beautiful, i.e. desirable. They travel long distances, wait for hours in the rain, in order to see her in the flesh, cheer themselves hoarse, and treasure her signature.

Alternatively an analytical mind may choose to regard this desirable thing as a complicated arrangement of blood and grease, constantly engaged in assimilating and defaecating living and dead matter, the seat of innumerable colonies of bacteria, exuding waste products through the skin that is intermittently covered with oleaginous hairs, impossible to maintain in a state of even approximate cleanliness.

Wherein lies the truth? Both views are evaluations, devoid of reality; the one is as true and as false as the other; the woman is what she is—not what other people choose to imagine her to be. But the reproduction of the species requires the positive illusion.

To perceive beauty in the form and colour of a film-star has no greater nor less justification than to perceive it in the form and colour of a hippopotamus, a baboon, or a tarantula. To perceive the ugliness in a toad, a hyena, or a scorpion has neither greater nor less justification than to perceive it in a film-star.

The degree of evolution of everyone may not allow him to conceive the external world as a percept of mind, but the minimum allows him to understand that human evaluations must be unreal.

The notion of the "charm" of human beings is pure vanity, fostered by journalism whose technique is insidious and perpetual flattery of all national and personal illusions.

32 ·- *Time and Space* - *VIII*

The Present

We never know the present because it is eternal (immobile). We can only know what we think of as the future when it has become what we think of as the past. The present is not in that illusory transformation at all. Not only do we not experience it: it is not there to be experienced.

The present is not within the time-sequence that we know, but that time-sequence may be within it.

33 ·- Reality and Manifestation - XI

Judge Not . . .

Wise men don't judge: they seek to understand.

Judging is an automatic response of the ego asserting itself: in so far as pure-intelligence (*buddhi*) has reduced the power of the ego the automatic response to stimulus is understanding.

The Buddha Nature (Bd.): The Atman (Ved.): The Father (Chr.)

The "I" is in every act—but not in its extinction.

The "I" is not an object, an other. I am not object (without), I am subject (within).

"I am . . ." is real, but the predicate (whatever it may be) is unreal.

There is only one reality that we can know: that reality is "I am."

Disciplines

What is the use of working to eliminate the manifestations of the ego (which is what is called discipline)?

You do not put out a light by hiding it behind a screen.

The treatment of symptoms does not cure a disease. Effects disappear when causes are removed, causes do not disappear when effects are suppressed.

Reduce the ego and its manifestations will vanish.

No action is right or wrong in itself, or by virtue of belonging to a category of actions so classed for purposes of social order.

Every action should be an adequate response to circumstances, whether that be slaughter or self-sacrifice.

Since our egos hinder us from responding adequately to circumstances we are well-advised to abide by the classification into "good" and "bad" devised for purposes of social order, but do not let us imagine that they are really such.

34 ⟿ Time and Space - IX

Eternity

That which is born dies. That which is not born cannot die. We do not think clearly in this matter. Some of us think that what is born may live "forever," but that is a concept dependent on the time-illusion. Our difficulty arises in conceiving anything that is not born.

We tend to conceive everything as subject to our notion of time. But "living for ever," i.e. going on living, is not the same thing as being eternal. The former is impossible, a pure illusion; the latter the only reality. Being eternal is never having been subject to the conception of time.

Being eternal is not "going on living": it involves no process of becoming: being eternal consists simply in Being.

35 · The Ego - II

Credo

I am aware of a relative "me" which I regard as a reflection of "I am" in the deforming time-mirror. Essentially separate from that relative "me" though emanating therefrom, I observe a purely artificial personality, an apparent artifact, built up by memory of all my reactions to my environment since birth. In this structure I am aware of no reality: I look upon it* as discontinuous, impermanent and multiple, that is divisible into different and often conflicting elements or "me"s. Whenever, or as long as, my relative "me," which, being relative, is based on reality and, on the phenomenal plane, is what is most really myself, is identified with my personality, which is an artifact of the imagination, I am a mechanical being and I suffer. If I were able to break that identification and to realise the fundamental identity of my relative self with my real self on the plane of Reality, which is at the same time Cosmic Mind, I should be free and know bliss. For it is evident that suffering is only possible owing to the dualistic circumstances of conflict on which and by means of which the personality appears to exist, and within the limitations which belief in it imposes upon my mind.

Suffering, in short, is exclusively confined to the ego, and I can only suffer in so far as I am identified with that.

---

* *Ed. Note:* i.e. the artificial personality

36 ⸱⁓ Brief Causeries – I

Enlightenment is straightly attained by freedom from separate selfhood.

—THE BUDDHA

Is not the idea of liberation in the domain of *maya*? Does not the Vedanta teach that the Atman (the I-reality) is always free? Why then should I struggle for my liberation?

—VIVEKANANDA

We have noted that this was the view of Ramana Maharshi (Ch. 28, *Reality and Manifestation IX*, p. 86). We can observe in several paragraphs of the brief Huang Po doctrine that Hsi Yun said the same thing. Is it not also implicit in Hui Neng?

But what are these people? Are they not precisely the outstanding, incontrovertible examples of men who lived, each in his way, for long years in a state of permanent illumination, the obvious *Jivan Muktas* of history?

They were speaking of what they knew from experience; their words do not excite controversy or arouse in us an expression of opinion; their words fall straight into our minds like stones thrown into a pond, clearly and definitely as (what we can recognise as) truth itself.

Beside them let us ask what is the value of the theories of metaphysicists and mystics who write *about* something they seek but have not found? These are opinions merely, interesting, stimulating, valuable as discussion among students, advanced students speaking to elementary students.

Let us be clear about the relative value of the two sources of knowledge. Moreover though both are necessarily expressed intellectually the latter are at best based on occasional intuitions, hastily seized and imperfectly interpreted, whereas the former are a direct and deliberate interpretation of knowledge from the plane on which intuition itself derives. And how simple and direct are the latter by comparison with the former! Is that not significative in itself?

Hui Neng, Ramakrishna, Ramana Maharshi, all realised their identity with Reality in early youth. None was at any time an intellectual. Each merely spoke to us in his own way from the plane on which he lived. Their verbal formulae differed, but the sense of their words is identical.

Do we know of any illuminated man, historically speaking, who realised his identity with Reality via an intellectual approach?

37 ·- Brief Causeries - II

Action and Non-Action, 3

The half-century during which Ramana Maharshi lived in a state of permanent Illumination (Liberation, Satori, identified with Reality) presents a remarkable picture of the dynamism of Non-Action.

From the records of his life (for instance *Les Etudes sur Ramana Maharshi,* by five or six eminent observers and Arthur Osborne's admirable biography) one does not have the impression that he was ever known to "act" in the sense in which that word is normally applied to human endeavour, that is in the sense of "do" which implies initiative and reaction. He was the living example of the philosophy of Lao Tzu. Even when attacked by ragamuffins, crooks, burglars, and hornets, he did not re-act; he rarely seems to have given orders, correction, or to have made plans, yet far from living in chaos and disorder his life and his ashram seem to have been a model of harmony and precision.

Only in the interim between his illumination at the age of sixteen and the emergence in him of a working-model of an ego for the purposes of human contact did he find it necessary to act, and those few recorded actions are worthy of study. From his life it would appear that the I-Reality does not, perhaps cannot, act or re-act on the plane of seeming, and that the dissolved ego being no longer available to that end, the living being remains negative to the circumstances of life. The Maharshi had no wishes, fear or anger; he merely did what he had to do with the directness and simplicity of a young child, illuminated by an intelligence of rare lucidity.

His real action—Adequate Action, as we may call it— which is Non-Action on the plane of Reality was in the medium of what we know as Silence. But such Silence was not the negative state we associate with that word; on the contrary it was highly positive, potent, dynamic. Constantly his "radiation" was felt, very occasionally "seen," and is even described as "terrific." Indeed for a number of people it appears to have been too powerful—like a high-voltage current. And by means of it he administered, directly to individuals, and generally to all, present and absent, what is adequately described as his Grace—which was his guidance, more effective than words, and which constituted his revelation.

His case, as far as one knows, is unique as a contemporary phenomenon experienced by innumerable people now living, many still young, but its importance may be regarded as a function of its uniqueness.

38 ·– Brief Causeries - III

"All the World's a Stage, and All the Men and Women Merely Players"

Is there a more apposite parable than that implied by the Maharshi comparing man and actor?

"All the actions that the body is to perform are already decided upon at the time it comes into existence: the only freedom you have is whether or not to identify yourself with the body."

David Garrick plays Othello or Romeo, Falstaff or Bottom, and identifies himself with his part; he loves and hates, saves and slays, laughs and weeps, but his part was decreed by Shakespeare; he plays it again and again, a hundred, a thousand times, and can only vary his interpretation without departing from the text. But he is David Garrick all the time; David Garrick is his reality, Othello or Falstaff is his role. Perhaps waiting in the wings between acts he remembers that he is really David Garrick, then when his cue comes he identifies himself again with his personage.

Man's role as an actor is cast when he comes onto the stage of manifestation and he has to play it out as it is written (by karma if you will) but he remains a man even while he is being an actor. His only freedom lies in whether he chooses to remember that he is also a man (Reality) in which case he is free and plays his part dispassionately by means of his acquired technique.

The analogy may apply even to the repetition of the part, for a hundred performances of a role by an actor may correspond to a hundred reincarnations of a man—"reincarnations" as popular religion would have it—"recurrences" as meta-psychologists may conceive it.

Does a man play his part in life better when he ceases to identify himself with his psycho-somatic apparatus and what that apparatus thinks, feels, and does—that is his role in life—and identifies himself instead with his I-Reality? We have been told that a man who has realised his state of satori is thereby a better coachman, chimney-sweep, lawyer, or ruler, and those who observed the Maharshi reported that everything he did was meticulously and accurately done, and that everything he said was simple, lucid, and impeccably expressed.

Does not an actor play his part better when he relies on his technique, retaining his self-identification and not identifying with his imaginary personage? Great actors are such, the others are what the French call *cabotins*.

39 ·- *Brief Causeries - IV*

Realisation by Non-Action

The extreme simplicity of the doctrines of the Maharshi and that of Huang Po, compared with the complexities of the religions into which each was born, is surely significant. This appears to some as a fault, whereas it is the very seal of their truth.

The doctrine of the Maharshi never varied over fifty years, and it had no development, demonstrating thereby the absence of intellectuality and the presence of reality. A philosophy evolves, it is an intellectual structure; the teaching of the Maharshi was merely the consignment of spiritual knowledge. And the difference between it and the doctrine of Hsi Yun is merely a difference of terminology.

When the most brilliant of his disciples died the Maharshi

was asked whether this man of immense intellectual stature could have attained realisation in this life, and he replied, "How could he? His *sankalpas* were too strong." *Sankalpas* are desires and ambitions, i.e. affectivity and intellectuality under the sway of the ego.

If the great religions are highly complex in their developed forms—that is through intellectual elaboration and spiritual discipline—we observe little trace of either in the doctrines of their Founders. It may be difficult to sift the recorded words that may reasonably be attributed to them from those placed in their mouths several centuries later, but what appears authentic in the earliest recorded form of their doctrine has considerable simplicity, whether it be attributed to Shri Krishna, the Buddha, or Jesus.

Why, then, do men and women elaborate these doctrines to the point at which they become in many respects the opposite of that which the Founders themselves preached?

It may be that when these doctrines were understood, which may have happened rapidly, it was observed that such comprehension had little noticeable effect and did not immediately produce illumination. Since such rapid understanding, save in one case in ten thousand, is almost entirely intellectual and hardly at all intuitive, this is clearly inevitable. So the disappointed but hopeful disciples, who keenly perceived the reality (truth) of the doctrine, started elaborating techniques (philosophies and disciplines) in order to transmute their simple understanding into realisation.

But it is doubtful whether such methods can often succeed in transmuting intellectual understanding into spiritual experience, and the later teachers do not encourage us to believe that they do. Rather do they suggest that there is no method—other than intuitive comprehension itself, and the elimination of the artificial ego which stands in the way. As long as we identify ourselves with that, with our psycho-somatic apparatus, instead of with our I-Reality, we cannot possibly realise anything, for realisation is precisely experiencing that shift of identification.

But the artificial ego cannot be eliminated by an act of will, nor can discipline dispose of it, since all such attempts are within *maya*, i.e. on its own plane and via itself (a thief, posing as a policeman in order to catch himself, as the Maharshi put it).

The suppression of pride, desire, anger, what you will, cannot destroy their cause. A malady cannot be cured by suppressing its symptoms. That is putting the wagon before the oxen. When the artificial ego is transcended, all its manifestations will automatically disappear. For that reason discipline must be futile.

Therefore detachment is the only method, and that is attained by understanding the falsity and futility of all the things on which the ego depends for its sustenance.

Only when that state of mind is attained is the way clear for the intuitive comprehension of the I-Reality and the transcendence of identification which in a flash raises a man or a woman to consciousness on the plane of Reality.

40 ·— Physics and Metaphysics – IX

The Frontier

The ultimate element of the Universe on the plane of dualism, as revealed by micro-physics (analysis of the atom), seems to consist of positive and negative charges of electrical energy (energy expressed as electricity). That, then, appears to be the basis of the universe perceived dualistically.

Positive and negative, as we have had occasion to observe, are—as in other pairs of opposites—obverse and reverse of a single coin. What, then, is this coin whose dualistic expression is positive and negative electricity?

The answer looks as though it should be Pure Energy. Is that yet another word for Cosmic Mind? Or is it an abstract concept denoting the aspect of Cosmic Mind when entering into Manifestation and before being perceived dualistically?

Man Is an Electronic Apparatus

Regarded from the point of view of physics the artificial ego is a non-conductor which insulates the current from the psyche. When this resistance is eliminated the *jivanmukta* receives the full amperage and his psyche is permanently incandescent.

That which manifests as light or heat in mechanical apparatus using electricity seems to be the gross manifestation of what we call *buddhi* in the liberated human being, and *buddhi* manifests as what we try to describe as "pure" intelligence and "pure" love (Caritas).

How many of the ways (disciplines, exercises, practices) recommended as helpful, or even necessary, for the attainment of Satori are not in fact *consequences* of that state erroneously suggested as *means*?

The integrated man, man made perfect, alone has attained a state of equilibrium in the process of living.

The Eye That Cannot See Itself, 2

"Realisation comes in search of us and we cannot go in search of Realisation." (Swami Siddheswarananda)

"You cannot choose Reality, it is Reality that must choose you." (Krishnamurti)

The Buddha, Hui Neng, Huang Po, Swami Vivekananda, Ramana Maharshi, Swami Siddheswarananda, Krishnamurti . . . N'insistons plus!

Benjamin Franklin likened the quest for God to searching a dark room for a black cat that isn't there. On that analogy the quest for Realisation may be likened to searching an unfurnished attic for a white cat that is sitting on the window-sill. Try calling "Puss, puss."

∝

"Followers of the Tao, there is no place in Buddhism for using effort, just be ordinary, without anything special." (Rinzai, Lin-chi)

This is an interesting detail of historical evidence (from the founder of the principal still-surviving school of Zen Buddhism, disciple of Hsi Yun of Huang Po, died A.D. 867), of the mixed heredity of Zen. He addresses his remark to followers of the Tao, but identifies himself with Buddhism, confirming historically what the doctrine suggests, that the original (pure) Taoism had survived in the Zen school of Buddhism.

The statement itself goes to join all those already quoted on the subject of Realisation.

41 ·~ *Brief Causeries - V*

Bliss

It seems clear, as Monsieur Linssen has explained to us, that what we call "love," with its possessivity, its sensuality, its essential egoism, is in fact the refraction in a denser medium of what he terms "divine love," that which manifests in the *jivanmukta* as impersonal *caritas* and which he has permanently as a state of mind. Manifesting in us through the artificial ego it is polluted by all the desires and avidities of that, and, becoming affective, acquires a shadow which never leaves it and which is suffering.

But the full implication of this has never been stated, as far as I am aware, perhaps because it seems too obvious to the wise men (those who make books); but we are not all wise, and happily we do not (quite) all write books.

It should be obvious that all our poor little motives, the dynamism of everything we do or think, of every action we ever take, of whatever nature, in short every single manifestation of which we are capable, is simply a refraction through our ego of an aspect of Reality.

We may be tired of hearing that what "is" on the plane of Reality becomes what "exists" on the plane of seeming, that the One becomes the many (or the "ten thousand things"), or that every phenomenon must have a noumenon; and anyhow that is usually just an intellectual conception.

We may be able to transmute that into intuitional understanding, into real knowledge, and assimilate it in experience, which is a gauge of enlightenment, if we come to realise it piecemeal instead of *en bloc*. To that end we may trace back each of our impulses to its noumenal state, and know what it is that is being misused and degraded in our psyche by the artificial ego in whose illusory power we are content to live in a state that most of us recognise as conflict and misery.

For instance, to quote Robert Linssen in this connection, speaking of a liberated man, "Comment pourrait-il en effet trouver un intéret quelconque dans la jouissance de quoi que ce soit, s'il goute à chaque instant, le 'Souverain Délice' de l'*Ananda*, qui suggère inlassablement le désir au coeur de tous les etres?"

In these words he tells us that it is *Ananda* (Bliss) on the noumenal plane that manifests phenomenally via our egos as desire for enjoyment. And we are made to see how futile and transitory are our enjoyments in comparison with the immensity of the Bliss of which they are a dim and fast-fading echo.

We can also perceive that without the artificial ego we could not desire these feeble and make-believe enjoyments—as artificial as the ego which seeks them—and that its elimination cannot but result in leaving us directly accessible to the noumenon of those desires—which is the state of mind called *Ananda* or Bliss.

There may be another side to this picture, one that indeed is always turned to the wall.

If all our poor little motives and desires, our pitiful little enjoyments, recognised as such, are really reflections or echoes of Bliss on the plane of Reality, as our deplorable egotistic "love" is a reflection of its reality, all of which are demonstrated in manifestation, direct and without refraction in the muddy waters of an ego, by liberated men (men liberated from their egos), then do we not malign them a little?

They may be poor relations, but they come of good stock.

The echoes may be feeble and confused, but the Voice is Harmony Itself. The shadows may be fugitive and transparent, but the Substance is Reality. If we trace them back to their origin we shall surely find Ourselves.

How much better than going and sitting on our haunches in a cave and regarding our navels as though there were something there to look at, which only results in cramp and hypnosis! If we do as I suggest we will be doing what the Zen Masters have been telling us to do for twelve hundred years, i.e. to seek realisation through living.

"When I am hungry I eat; when I am tired I lie down."

Since our every sensation is an evidence of Reality, and since it is Reality that we seek to real-ise, a path opens before us in every moment of our lives.

Instead of spurning our desires and avidities, and our little pleasures, on account of their recognisable futility and egoism, we might advantageously lead them up the garden-path so that they may introduce us to the source of their being.

42 ·- Work and Play - VI

Love, 1

Love itself is intemporal. Only the *jivanmukta* (libéré vivant) knows it in its plenitude, and he lives in it. Probably only those who have experienced the effulgence of such a one have known it even at second hand, though it may perhaps be experienced temporarily by people in some *samadhis* or ecstasies. What we know as love is perhaps a reflection of that in muddy water darkened by the contents of our ego and misapplied to desire—desire for possession and sensual desire. In so far as any of us may be capable of *caritas* we may have the clearest reflection of it that is possible on the plane on which we normally live.

Our experience of love is affective: love itself is *buddhi*—a ray of Reality. We have been led to regard *buddhi* as what we think of as Pure Intelligence. No doubt it is that, but it should also be Pure Emotion, equally devoid of thought and of affectivity. It is what-it-is, but in order to conceive it we need to envisage both aspects.

"Union"

Human love is a will-o'-the-wisp. How could any human being either possess or unite with another? Psychically, there is nothing possessible to possess, nothing dispossessible to give, nothing with which to effect union. Physically, contact of surfaces is only juxtaposition, and no simulation of penetration can ever go deeper than surfaces.

Whatever we may do we find a surface opposed to another surface.

On the plane of Manifestation each of us is utterly separate and alone. Union is only on the plane of Reality, and thereon mutual possession is universal and absolute.

Our notion of love is perhaps a nostalgia for that.

Self-sacrifice? . . . If only it were possible!

What we think of as self-sacrifice has been described as the supreme form of selfishness.

43 ·~ Reality and Manifestation - XII

The integrated man, he in whom equilibrium has been re-established, has no wishes. As with love so is it with desires; freed from the personal factor, the one has become *caritas* and the other a glad acceptance that what must happen shall happen.

Ends as Means

As one comes to understand the consequences of Satori he splits them up, in his normal manner of the plane of seeming, into what he discriminates as qualities, attributes, character-istics, whereas they are one whole state in Reality.

These qualities he seeks, perhaps unconsciously but often by disciplining his ego, to practise in his existing condition, having imagined those consequences as means. This process seems to resemble a species of sympathetic magic, as prac-tised in Central Africa.

But can there be any virtue in it? Imagining the greatest conceivable degree of success, will the result be anything but an imitation, a mimicry, an actor playing the role of a god? Even if it became habitual through conditioned reflexes the subject of such conditioning would remain in the same iden-tification as before the process began. Could a conditioned ego bring him nearer the realisation of the state he imitates? It seems unlikely, and perhaps even less than in the case of purely intellectual understanding, less because it may consti-tute a barrier, or should one say a greater barrier?

Progress?

How *proud* you are of your humility!

How you *enjoy* self-sacrifice!

How *devoted* you are to detachment! (Except, of course, when you are *indifferent*.)

How *grateful* you are to yourself for being kind to others!

∽

Every time we use the word "ego" we are talking nonsense. Do we realise that?

Self Is Not Self

The Self is not my-self, your-self; it is only ITS-self—the Self of the essence of the universe.

"There is no self but the Self": i.e. *there IS no my-self or your-self.*

Rather than anything personal the Self is Suchness, Thusness, Quiddité. It is only applicable to a thing or an animal in so far as such thing or animal represents the Absolute.

Our identification of it with that which is personal is no doubt the essence of our false identification with a supposed ego.

If we realised that we had no self we should at the same time realise the true meaning of the word. That might be the essential of intuitive knowledge.

"Find Out Who It Is Who Is Predestined or Has Free Will" (Ramana Maharshi)

"Whatever is destined not to happen will not happen, try as you may. Whatever is destined to happen will happen, do what you may to prevent it. This is certain."

"All actions that the body is to perform are already decided upon at the time it comes into existence: the only freedom you have is whether or not to identify yourself with the body."

Probably you did not believe me? (*Freewill and Reality*, Ch. 18). You might consider more worthy of consideration the words of someone speaking from the plane of Reality, and rightly so. The words quoted were written, and spoken, by the Maharshi.

But, since this is not a collection of quotations, but an independent transmission with its own turn of thought, however lacking in authority, I will give it in the words of this pilgrim:

You cannot do that which is already left undone: nor can you not do that which already is done.

44 ·- Work and Play - VII

Love, 2

The positive and negative elements, in the form known as masculinity and femininity, two aspects of a single manifestation, are in a state of imbalance in male and female respectively, each manifesting an excess of one element.

The association of male and female has the apparent effect of restoring this double imbalance to a state of equilibrium. Since the attainment of equilibrium is constantly and automatically sought throughout manifestation the mutual attraction of male and female, and the mutual need of one another, thereby becomes comprehensible.

But it is a need that can never attain fulfilment during life, nor anything but a simulation thereof. From this there results all sexual performances on the one hand, and all specific conflict between the sexes on the other.

Contact of male and female, regardless of age or condition, always and inevitably constitutes an attempt at the reunion of separated elements and the re-establishment of a disturbed equilibrium.

But this process of contact may well constitute reunion in another dimension, temporarily at least, which is represented by a subtle relationship on the plane of manifestation that is described by terms such as romantic and sentimental.

But every such contact, between individuals (more accurately described as force-fields), however separated by circumstances and unknown to one another, may constitute a union on the plane that is beyond the apprehension of our senses.

The more dynamic and less impermanent examples of this universal process are somewhat inappropriately called "love."

45 ·~ *Reality and Manifestation - XIII*

Wake Up!

There seem to be two kinds of searchers: those who seek to make their ego something other than it is, i.e. holy, happy, unselfish (as though you could make a fish unfish), and those who understand that all such attempts are just gesticulation and play-acting, that there is only one thing that can be done, which is to disidentify themselves with the ego, by realising its unreality, and by becoming aware of their eternal identity with pure Being. That is just coming out of the waking dream such as nightly we come out of the sleeping dream.

Is it not fatuous to criticise what people do, since they have to do it? The only thing we can criticise without being ridiculous is their identification which obliges them to be automats.

Many of us know, are convinced *intellectually*, that our bodies are unreal but nevertheless ninety-nine per cent of our thoughts and actions are based on the belief in their reality, i.e. in their apparent reality, that what our senses tell us about them is real. That is perhaps a fair measure of the gap between intellectual understanding and real knowledge.

What of those of us who have come to conceive of them as force-fields in continual flux? Do we think we have arrived at a concept that has one foot in phenomenal science and the other in Reality?

Until we have known Liberation can we hope to be free of that identification with the psycho-somatic apparatus? Until we are free of that identification can we hope to know Liberation?

But that amounts to saying, "Until we have abandoned that identification can we hope to abandon that identification?"

Surely the answer is that they are one and the same phenomenal experience and therefore simultaneous, for in order effectively to abandon identification we must no longer exist (psychologically).

❧

The normal in Physics is the point of view of the majority. The normal in Metaphysics is the point of view that *should be* that of the majority.

❧

The wise man knows too much not to know that he knows nothing.

46 ·~ *Work and Play - VIII*

Les Primaires

The primary intelligence does not know how to discuss. It only knows how to argue. And argument as far as it is concerned is a contest which it must "win" at all costs. Instead of seeking to extract the maximum of meaning from the statements of others the primary intelligence seeks to refute everything it hears.

This inadequate utilisation of the mind is even more clearly defined when the subject matter is personal. Whereas a controlled mind will receive personal criticism with interest, even with eagerness, seeking to benefit by any truth it may be able to recognise in the criticism—since it is inevitably difficult for human beings to regard themselves dispassionately, so that the criticism of others can be of great value—the primary intelligence will fight back at once, using any argument, however inadequate, that comes to hand, and without any reasoning other than self-defence, self-justification, or offence (*tu quoque*).

Thus it becomes virtually impossible for the primary intelligence to learn anything from discussion, particularly concerning itself. Strange as it may seem this condition can be observed even in people who, otherwise, have quite a high standard of culture.

One would have thought that the first object of education should be to remove this obstacle to mental development. But education seems to be more concerned with effects than with causes, much as primitive medicine is more concerned with symptoms than with their origins.

47 ·~ Physics and Metaphysics - X

Silence, 1

The Maharshi seems to have been the first human being to use silence deliberately and to have rendered such use comprehensible. At any rate if there is a trace of its use in the East or the West, in the distant or recent past, such use seems to have been unrecognised and nowhere understood or expounded.

Nor was the use of silence immediately understood in the entourage of the Maharshi. It was and still is said that he gave no *upadesa* (instruction), because he did not lecture. In fact he did give considerable verbal instruction, probably against his better judgement, in order to placate the exigencies of his followers, but his real *upadesa* was given by means of silence.

The Zen Masters never ceased to make it clear that verbal instruction, since language is necessarily dualistic, is useless and does more harm than good. Hence their *mondo* and *koans.* The Buddha denounced "discoursing." And the transmission of the *Dharma*, from Patriarch to Patriarch, was given by silence.

What, then, is this method or technique of silence? It uses silence rather than is silence, and, no doubt, only by, or in, silence can it be explained.

A key to its understanding would seem to lie in the notion of "grace," and the chief thing that we know of it is that it is more potent than speech. Those who have had long experience of it can make us realise its immense power, but little of its mechanism.

At least we can open our minds to its reality, and seek to understand it. We find ourselves in an unknown land. The vistas that open up before us exceed all expectations. Silence, which we thought of as a negative state, devoid of interest, is seen to be a positive and dynamic mode of being.

The Suddenness of Satori

There exists an elementary confusion about the "sudden" character of satori—the so-called "sudden" as opposed to "gradual" schools of Zen (those of Hui Neng and of Shen-hsiu).

But there is not, never was and never could be, anything sudden about satori except the event itself, i.e. the "turning-over" (*paravritti*) of the mind—and that is necessarily instantaneous—a seizure of the present. Its preparation may be considered to require untold millions of our years. Regarded within the framework of our lifetime that preparation may be short or long, may be fulfilled in youth or old-age—on the rare occasions on which it is fulfilled at all. There is nothing sudden about the preparation of satori, but the event itself appears to be both unexpected and immediate.

Suddenness is a function of Time. Satori is an intemporal state. The time-factor (our notion of time) is quite inapplicable to it.

Preparation for Satori

There is no Path to Satori. It cannot be attained. As we have seen, all the Masters tell us that we cannot seize Reality: it is Reality that seizes us. And we must not strive for it, because Mind cannot be reached through mind.

But we can prepare ourselves for it. This preparation consists in attaining—attainment is on the plane of phenomena—a state of consciousness in which as many hindrances as possible are removed, a state of relative *dépouillement*, so that we shall be *en disponibilité*, so that Reality may be able to seize us if It will.

Let me put it like this. In the hierarchy of the Catholic Church there is only one Pope among many million members, and he is chosen from among many dozens of cardinals. There is no path to papacy, direct or indirect, but there is a path to the condition of cardinalcy. Arrived at the state of member of the Sacred College a man is no surer of the papal state than he was on the day he was born, but he is *papabile*— he could be chosen.

Nothing he himself can "do" will lead him to the papal state: that depends on factors outside his control, largely imponderable and innate factors. And, to make the parable more exact, there have been rare instances when the Pope has been selected from outside the cardinalcy and even from outside the priesthood.

But is not the status of a cardinal an end in itself? Is it not already much? Is it not to a great extent its own reward?

Neither the papal state nor the realisation of the state of

satori is generally our lot, though both are available to all men. We do not strive to become Pope, we must not strive to become Jivan Muktas. But we may attain the state of *disponibilité* by striving—and that state is its own reward (even if such reward does not include the ego-affirmation of wearing a nice red hat).

I have said that the state of "papability," of *disponibilité*, may be striven for. What is it, and how?

Surely it is just understanding, intellectual at first, transmuted into intuitional knowledge. When we have sufficiently disposed of ignorance, knowledge may take its place, and when we have knowledge the artificial ego evaporates, dies of inanition, and our relative Reality is ready for integration with Reality Itself. Then we are at the disposal of the Absolute.

48 · Reality and Manifestation - XIV

Silence, 2

Upadesa is verbal teaching, teaching by means of a dualistic instrument (language), which cannot hope to do more than suggest the truth and which, owing to its inherent limitations, at the same time obscures it.

But in silence Pure Intelligence can function directly and with immediacy, unhindered even by Time. Its potency is incomparable.

Choice

Why chose? Why not just do what you have to do anyhow? Not to choose is "d'être présent dans le Présent."

Our whole life as prisoners of the personal illusion is a series of choices. From morning till night we do nothing but choose.

If we ceased to choose and just responded to circumstances that would be to act in accordance with the "true nature of things." But that is what the integrated do.

Yes, we choose from morning till night, yet there is no such thing as choice.

Silence, 3

Whoever has studied the *mondo* of the Zen Masters has noted with surprise and mystification tales, of different periods and different sages, according to which a pupil after years of residence in a monastery goes to the master in profound discouragement, tells him how long he has been with him and asks when he may hope to begin receiving some instruction. At which the Master turns in apparent astonishment and says something such as "But you have brought me my tea every day!"

Few, if any, of us have understood. Rather have we thought how strange and different the Chinese must be, patiently to spend years without being taught anything.

Then perhaps we have come across the tale of the pupil who lived for years with an old master in the hope of being taught "intemporal" swordsmanship, serving him day and night in his house. Whenever he asked for instruction he received a blow with a stick. Then one day, in exasperation, while the old man is bending over the fire poking the embers, he seizes a stick and tries to bring it down on his master's shoulders. But the old master, without looking round, without seeing what is happening, swings the poker over his head, wards off the blow and continues his business with the fire.

The pupil has understood in a flash.

What a silly story, we say! Or do we too see in a flash the meaning of these symbolic tales?

But if we come to study the life of the Maharshi, which is almost to live with him in his ashram, we observe the whole process in operation. There, too, there are people who complain that they receive no instruction—although the Maharshi answered more questions in plain dualistic language than any Zen master ever seems to have done. But we also perceive that the disciples are receiving instruction during twenty-four hours of each day, and we come to understand that this instruction is more real and immeasurably more potent than any discursive, and so necessarily false, teaching could ever be. Thus *we* also have understood.

49 ·~ *Physics and Metaphysics - XI*

Satori, 4

The statement of Zen that "Every perception is an opportunity for satori" should perhaps be taken in conjunction with the phrase "The eye cannot see itself."

Reality is ubiquitous, but also, as Robert Linssen tells us, "Elle est au centre même de notre faculté de perception."

The eye that sees, the ear that hears, the tongue that tastes are only apparatus, but the I that sees, hears and tastes is Reality. We only need to realise that and the first perception becomes satori.

❧

The eye that cannot see itself is the I that cannot conceive itself.

Sex

In so far as masculine and feminine are positive and negative electrically we may remember that positively charged particles repel one another, negatively charged particles likewise, whereas positively and negatively charged particles attract one another. This aspect of sexual relations needs no exposition.

Stereoscopic Thinking (ref. *Reality and Manifestation - X, Logic and Superlogic,* Ch. 29)

Swami Siddeswarananda offers a simile so apposite that it seems more than a mere metaphor: it has something of the character of a symbol. He compares the outlook of a man who has attained realisation with stereoscopic vision.

We look at a couple of duodimensional pictures, two slightly different aspects of an object, and then place them in the apparatus which unites them in focus, and immediately we behold an image that has the quality of a third dimension.

In everyday life our two eyes receive each a duodimensional image which, combined in focus in our brain, gives us a tridimensional picture. One may suppose that the duplication of our sense-organs has this effect as its primary function—in the interest of our protection and efficiency.

Leaving the sensory plane of percepts for the intellectual

plane of concepts, we conceive everything dualistically, that is to say everything is conceived as relatively good-bad, hot-cold, light-dark, new-old, but never can we conceive one and the same thing as possessing both characteristics at once, never can we—as on the perceptual plane—see the image from two aspects simultaneously. Well-water at, say, sixty degrees that seems cool in summer, at the same temperature seems warm in winter. In spring and autumn it may seem neither cool nor warm, but never can we conceive it as both. A man or a woman may seem to us to be what we call "good" or "beautiful" one day and what we call "bad" or "ugly" the next, while on a third day he or she may seem to be neither, but on no occasion will he seem to be both at once.

We have an emotionally positive concept of someone or something, and an emotionally negative concept; at one moment we like someone or something, at another we dislike that person or thing, but never the two at the same time. Were we to discover a means of blending these two tridimensional mental concepts should not the resulting concept automatically have the quality of a further dimension?

If the so-called "opposites" are really complementaries must they not be capable of blending by focus in a stereoscopic vision, acquiring thereby that further dimension which reveals reality?

For at such a moment we should no longer be thinking dualistically.

Presence in the Present

Every time you watch yourself doing something, perceiving something, you are transcending yourself.

Every time you stand outside yourself (transcend yourself) you leave the river of time and swim ashore. You are on the bank watching time flow past. But, as has already been said, an element of us is always on the bank—otherwise we could not be conscious that time flows. Therefore what really happens when we transcend ourselves is that we transfer our identification from the fictitious entity to the I that is relative to Reality.

But in so far as I partake of Reality I am in the Present, the present which is No-Time, observing the illusory process of "future" turning into "past."

That seems to be the only way in which the non-integrated can approach the state of Presence in the Present, for that is the state of the integrated and a consequence of Realisation, and a consequence cannot be used as a means.

To attempt to seize the present via the fictitious entity is to seek to bring that fictitious entity into the Presence of the Present. That is to attempt to bring the illusory into the presence of the Real.

When we deliberately endeavour, by some kind of act of discipline, that is by "will," that is by means of the ego-mechanism, to seize the present we are merely fixing our attention on the more recent past.

50 ·- Work and Play - IX

Love, 3

The average person is not able to conceive of "love" apart from the desire for possession. In his, or her, perspective the desire for possession is the test of "love," the touchstone by which its "sincerity" or "reality" is gauged. Even a mother who is not possessive towards her child is accused of not "loving" him, of being a "bad" mother, whereas she alone is a "good" one. Not only could he not understand that desire for possession is incompatible with love, but he could not recognise as "love" a sentiment in which it was not present. But the fact is that love is not a sentiment at all but a state of mind, and what he calls "love" is not love—for "love" is a violent manifestation of the artificial ego, and love is love in the degree in which the element of self is transcended.

He who may not understand this can try to imagine a state of mind in which he is conscious of a profound but unemotive love for a chosen object—for "love," the sentiment, and love, the non-affective, are infused by the same force and basically are identical, the one covered in egoistic debris and slime, the other *dépouillé* and pure.

He can try to imagine the total elimination of the desire for possession of the chosen object, understanding that possession is anyhow an impossibility and can never be more than a psychological complex of projections, attachments, and exigencies. He can envisage the possibility of expecting nothing from the chosen object, demanding nothing, not even the physical presence of that object—for love, having an intemporal and non-spatial character, is not dependent on physical presence or sensual contact. Jealousy must cease to be conceivable in this perspective, and no sense of personal injury can find a place.

"But this is an exclusively 'spiritual' relationship?" "Spiritual" if the word seems useful, but why exclusively? Purely, if he wishes, in the etymological sense of the word. For the discrimination between spiritual and physical is illusory; they are two aspects of one and the same reality. Physical expression of love is in no way excluded; it may even be an essential element in the relationship, a culmination, the vital expression, since the relationship is on the plane of phenomena.

But in this case the ego remains in abeyance.

The state of mind that is love is self-sufficient. Its actualisations on the plane of phenomena are fulfilments of a cathartic character, psychic and physical.

Promises

At the most a promise is an expression, at a given moment, of a desire, seen as intention, to carry out the action promised. At the least it is a children's game of "Let's Pretend" played by adults who take it seriously.

Since, in our present state (conditioned by conditioned reflexes), we are the unconscious "victims" of an intricate mechanism that goes by the name of cause-and-effect and can only do what we must, it makes little difference whether we know that we know what we have to do, whether we suspect that we know what we have to do, or whether we are totally unaware that we know it.

It is inevitable that we know it, since we have done it again and again in the beginningless and endless circuit of the time-process which we see as future-into-past, but which from the dimension at right-angles is a composite present.

To promise to do something which we must do anyhow is meaningless. To promise to do something that may not be, or is not, what we must do, is not only meaningless but sets up a conflict between what we think we want to do and what we have to do, a futile conflict, since ultimately we can only want what we must, and this conflict represents an attempt to obtain what we want by doing something that we are not able to do, or, if you prefer, an attempt to want one thing and obtain the result that could only come from another.

A promise, therefore, is devoid of significance; it cannot have any part in reality. It is no more than a form of words which in no circumstances can express more than the desire or sentiment which actuates us at a given moment.

To make a promise in all seriousness presupposes the notion that we are free to do as we will at any given moment, which is manifestly absurd, and which only ignorance and incomprehension could allow us to suppose. Knowing this, to make a promise is either dishonest or just a conventional form of words to express a sentiment. To try to "keep" a promise, or to try to oblige another to do so, is as futile as trying to stop the tide from coming in because you want to keep your feet from getting wet. . . .

∾

We are as unable to change anything but ourselves as Canute was when he tried, or pretended to try, to arrest the tide on the sea-shore. Our only liberty is in the dimension "within." If we can change our selves then everything must change as far as our circuit in time is concerned. But opportunities to do that are not readily seized, and they are generally provided by another human being since few of us can change our selves by our selves. The illusory self cannot affect our position on the wheel of recurrence, for an illusion by definition is powerless to affect anything. But in so far as that illusory self may be modified, reduced or extinguished we can escape an invariable recurrence and alter our "lives" within the time-process, for a helicoidal movement is thereby created in a further dimension—that in which all possibilities exist.

132

Sacrifice: A Quatrain

1. There is only one person to whom you can sacrifice yourself.

2. There is only one thing that we can sacrifice, and that is our self. And we cannot make that sacrifice too often. Or too completely.

3. An action that does not comprise sacrifice of one's self is not worth taking, for it is cut off from reality, and is not anything.

4. Sacrifice that involves an act of will is not a sacrifice of, but an affirmation of, the self. Sacrifice of the self, on the contrary, is a *lâcher-prise*, a *surrender*.

Afterthought. Anything one does for oneself is not worth doing.

Love and Sex: A Geometrical Concept

Let us visualise love as a great light. When its source is close to the lens—the screen or prism, as we have called it, which cuts us off from direct access to Reality—the light is evenly distributed throughout the whole field of vision; it is a luminous flood, all-embracing, bathing all alike in its radiance.

But in the measure in which the lens is withdrawn from the source this great light becomes concentrated into a beam and is focused on one object at a time.

The former is impersonal love, sometimes called divine love, or *caritas*. The latter is exemplified by the love of a man for a woman.

In this image we perceive that there are not different kinds of love, but that love is one whole thing, and that the apparent differences in its manifestations are a question of focus.

❧

The manifestation of the sexual urge follows a similar pattern. It appears to be a related force but manifesting in a denser medium. The force that was psychic in expression is here predominantly physical. But the image holds good.

On the animal plane, as a physiological necessity, the sexual urge is unfocused, without discrimination, impersonal. But as the lens is withdrawn from the source of the energy the beam becomes concentrated on objects and appears ultimately as a ray that is focused on one object only.

But it is a psychic factor that withdraws the lens in both cases, and in the measure in which the lens is withdrawn, and the beams are concentrated on objects, the related forces appear to coalesce until in the "explosion" of coition they seem to unite.

So to visualise this mechanism enables us to see in perspective the phenomena to which we tend to attribute so much importance, such as "fidelity" and "infidelity" in sexual relations, "promiscuity," etc., etc.

It enables us to live in harmony with these related forces, and to use them for our happiness instead of tending, as we do, to struggle with them in a dark room as unknown and invisible enemies.

This image in itself is inadequate, however, because it is over-simplified. It is a simple rectilinear image—and nothing in the universe can be supposed to be rectilinear (not even light, as Einstein demonstrated). And it is a tridimensional image—and nothing in the universe can be supposed to be tridimensional. But if we cannot, and we cannot, visualise a

134

quadridimensional image (save in mathematical symbols) we can at least conceive things as spherical.

So conceived the dual processes can be more adequately visualised, but in order to visualise them as in fact they may be we would need to endeavour to conceive the multiplication of the sphere within itself (in a further dimension within itself) and in the measure in which we may be able to do that—if we are able to do it at all—we may approach that accurate vision which otherwise can only be represented symbolically and in numbers.

Revaluation of Values, 2

When a beggar renders you the service of accepting a shilling he thanks you for giving him the opportunity of rendering you that service.

La vue juste, correct or true vision, requires a revaluation of values, of all values—as Nietzsche put it in a somewhat different context. The so-called "living by Zen" or "Zen way of life or of thinking" is no doubt just that. Such revaluation of values, of current values, is the gauge whereby the degree of comprehension of any pilgrim on the Way may be judged.

The statement in the first paragraph presents one such revaluation. Does it appear nonsense, just queer, or obvious? By that you may assess your degree of understanding.

Revaluation of values must be applied to everything within the reach of the mind; nothing has a right to escape it, from the most abstruse speculation down to the apparent facts and circumstances of the daily life that goes on around us, domestic, social, political.

When you hear someone speaking in all earnestness of the benefits of industrialisation, of social services, of democracy, of the standard of living, of works of public utility, of progress—whatever sense or meaning may be implied by any of these terms, or of abstract notions such as Justice, Liberty, Nationalism, Equality, do you think of them as real things or do you smile?

If you take them seriously and judge them you are accepting them as values. But if you have come to revalue values then you perceive their total unreality. You do not judge them as "good" or "desirable," you do not judge them as "bad" or "harmful," you do not judge them as anything in themselves, you merely perceive that they are not anything at all. They are what children do so seriously with boxes of bricks under the dining-room table. Very serious matters in their eyes, very unimportant indeed in yours. Our values change as we grow up.

Revaluation of values automatically results from comprehension of the unreal. Comprehension of the unreal is an indirect perception of Reality. Reality cannot be positively comprehended. It can never be expressed in dualistic language. It can only be approached by negation. But that is true Discrimination, the only Discrimination that can be so called, and it is *la Vue Juste* or True Vision.

Note: It should not be impossible for a pilgrim on the way who had comprehended the need for such a revaluation of values—and only a pilgrim could do so—to take part on the plane of seeming in the activities implied by the terms in question. He could discriminate regarding these notions, but it should not be possible for him to see them as "desirable" without at the same time seeing them as, and in the same degree, "undesirable" (for so they must necessarily be). He would in fact be taking part in the children's game of bricks under the dining-room table as any of us might do, as seriously as he could, but his tongue could never be far removed from his cheek.

Nationalism

There are no nations: there are only nationalisms.

Nor is there any such thing as a public, other than as a concept in the mind of a politician, an editor, a theatre, art or other "director," a dualistic concept whose inevitable falsity is regularly duplicated on the plane of experience.

By "nationalisms" is meant sentiments of a nationalistic character, perfectly imaginary and devoid of any kind of reality, and, by inference, large groups of individuals whose common feature is that they are a prey to this illusion.

Definition of Civilisation

Civilisation is based on a sort of stabilisation of egoisms in equilibrium.

When the balance is definitely upset the civilisation crumbles.

51 ·- Time and Space - X

Reincarnation and Recurrence, 3

Cassandra. Dogmas are ulcers in the bodies of religion in which are concentrated matter that is foreign and unfit for retention. But myths are symbols of something that is real. In myths a popular story, incredible in itself, and that cannot resist analysis, conceals a fundamental verity. One such is Reincarnation which is a myth that conceals the reality of Recurrence.

Another is that of the Trojan lady Cassandra, daughter of Priam, who could perceive the "future" as clearly as the "past," but who was never believed. The myth forbears to tell us that we are all Cassandras; at any rate where our own "futures" are concerned—Cassandras all. Those few of us who know it know also how painful it is, and we feel the deep pathos of the tragic life of the Trojan woman as each opportunity, that we have foreseen, is neglected despite all our efforts to make it clear to those we love.

Shakespeare knew it, too, when he told us that there is a tide in the affairs of men which, taken at the flood, leads on to fortune, but, neglected, leaves us to wallow in the shallows of misery. He, too, had watched that happening.

And then, one day, perhaps, we come to understand, and the meaning of the myth becomes clear.

We can no more seize those opportunities, so clearly seen, than a tram labelled "Balham" can take us to "Hamstead." Of course the points can be changed, but the driver, the ego in control, cannot do that; an independent intelligence has to be invoked.

When one has understood—it is no longer a tragedy to be Cassandra.

"From the Beginning Nothing Exists" (Hui Neng)

Louis de Broglie and Schrödinger, crowning half a century's work in physics, seem to have demonstrated mathematically and in the laboratory that there is nothing real that exists, nothing absolute that could exist. Mass appears to be only resistance to change (to movement of energy), decreasing in bulk in accordance with acceleration and increasing proportionally in energy. Matter, therefore, has no existence as such.

Hui Neng seems to have known that about 1300 years ago. Scientists have now demonstrated it. Wise men believed Hui

Neng; the unwise will believe the scientists.

Cause and Effect: The Result of What Hasn't Happened

There can be no such thing as a Cause, for the idea of causation presupposes the objective existence of Time. Cause-and-effect therefore are an illusion appertaining to the plane of seeming.

It follows that all theological, philosophical, metaphysical, and other rationalistic notions are attempts to explain what by means of our media of explanation must necessarily and forever be inexplicable.

52 ·- Work and Play - X

Revaluation of Values, 3

Giving something to somebody, helping anybody to obtain or do anything he wants, is gratifying the fictitious self of that person and affirming its power over him. Therefore so to do is to render him a disservice.

You can only render a service to somebody, and the only service you can render anybody, is to give him an opportunity of depriving himself of something, and of weakening the stranglehold of his fictitious self thereby.

In the first case the subject will thank you for rendering him a disservice, in the second case he will bear you a grudge for rendering him a service. Unless he happens to understand.

If you make a sacrifice for somebody you are serving yourself and doing an injury to your victim. If you accept a sacrifice you are suffering an injury and conferring a benefit.

But on the plane of Reality there is nothing to make a sacrifice, and no sacrifice that can be made, for love and sacrifice are no longer two things, and there is nothing else.

53 ·- Time and Space - XI

Parallelism of Lives

The Zen masters made it clear to us that we must "die to the past"; the Lankavatara Sutra, which, with the Diamond Sutra, constitutes the Buddhist basis of Zen, explains the disastrous role of habit-memory in anchoring us to the fictitious self which finds therein its principle source of power. What Robert Linssen terms "Présence au Présent" is the state of enlightenment itself. Let us hope that we have all come to understand that.

But the Zen masters show little sign of having understood the nature of time. Let us, therefore, seek to interpret this essential concept in the time-context. The past does not exist as such, neither past nor future can be passed or to come— for nothing is either "before" or "after" anything else. That, the time-sequence, is merely a phenomenal illusion, a product of our receptive mechanism. We visualise time-as-the-fourth-dimension-of-Space as best we may—that is spatially. Perhaps we use the analogy of the runway lights, seen one after the other from the aeroplane that is gathering speed, but seen simultaneously in a pattern when the further dimension of height has been gained.

But we can approach more nearly to reality than that, even

though ultimately it should be necessary entirely to discard a spatial concept: the notion of parallel lives is surely a clearer reflection of the truth.

Ouspensky seems to have sensed this, though he never—to my knowledge—developed the intuition, preferring the already admirable, and ancient, concept of recurrence in time. But surely the nearer-truth is that we live lives parallel to the one of which we are conscious from moment to moment. Every moment of our lives should be parallel to every other, so that we live every moment of our lives simultaneously. We do not live again and again in circles of time, as Ouspensky—and no doubt Pythagoras—suggested. We are not reborn every seventy odd years in the same conditions (period, place, and circumstances), repeating every detail of our lives unless we have been able to change our selves and evolve in a further dimension; rather *are we* living every detail of our lives at the same time on parallel planes.

In this there may seem to be two concepts apparently confused: parallelism of each moment as it enters consciousness, that is parallelism of the time sequence itself, and simultaneity of every moment of the complete time-sequence of a life. In this apparent confusion two different dimensions are involved, at right-angles to one another, in which a single phenomenon is envisaged from two different angles.

Of the dimension in which the simultaneity of a complete life is visualised I know of nothing to say, save that it is difficult for us to conceive, but the dimension in which we are living in parallel to ourselves at this, and every, moment is nearer and may more readily be visualised. Indeed it may merely be the fourth.

The Shape of Life

Let us methodically construct a geometrical representation of what should be a life in the phenomenal aspect of Reality.

We start with our usual and primary notion of a life as horizontal tram-line arbitrarily starting at a point "B" (birth) and ending suddenly at another point "D" (death). We recognise at once the absurdity of this, for no such horizontal straight line exists phenomenally, not even traced by light; so we curve it over into a circle. Then we realise that it must also exist in the dimensions at right-angles, that our conception of "before" and "after" is equally an "above" and "below," a "right" and "left," and we curve these over into circles also. But none of these circles has a beginning or end, and a circle springs from every present moment on every point of each of them.

Our figure has already become too complicated to be readily drawn or even conceived, so let us simplify it. We will visualise it as a wheel, with an infinite number of spokes, and the present moment is not on the circumference but is the axis round which this wheel of life revolves; it is eternal and it is perpetual movement at one point. Moreover identical wheels revolve round the same axis in every dimension, and their number is infinite, like their spokes. What we are now looking at is, in simplification, a sphere, a sphere whose elements, infinite in number, are revolving round the axis which is the now of any life. That which we recognise as "passed" or "to come" is any point on every spoke of every one of these wheels, whether seen as "above" and "below," "before" and "after," to "right" and "left"—which are appellations only, and each such point, repeated on every spoke, is itself the centre of a sphere.

What are the implications of this representation of a life?

First that the Present, eternal, is the axis and dynamic centre of everything in that life, that it, though movement at one point, itself has Immobility, though the source of action, itself is Non-Action. Second that, as we already know, there is no past or future, nothing "passed" or "to come," that everything that "has been" or "will be" is eternally "there" (regarded spatially in a spatial diagram), that every present moment creates its own "past" and "future" so that what we know as "past" and "future" are eternally around us in every "direction," that is "above *and* below," "before *and* behind," to "right *and* to left" of us, contemporary, simultaneous, here, and now. And we are living them all.

Thirdly, it follows from this that we can alter what we call past and future at every moment, but only by changing ourselves. This process, in those of us in whom it occurs in an appreciable degree, is a gradual one, usually dependent on others, from which we may conclude that our so-called past and future change rarely and by degrees.

Perhaps the answer to most of the questions that depend upon Time is to be found within this framework, and in a manner that ultimately is really very simple? All that may be needed is to visualise this representation, and to look.

This way of visualising a life incidentally reveals the identity of the I and the Now. If we are able to realise either we have at the same time realised both, for I-Reality and Now are One.

143

Past and Future, 2

What we call "the past" is a memory-impression of the present, of what "was," and still is, present. Yes.

Memory-impressions become increasingly transformed by the image-making faculty every time they are brought back into consciousness.

What we call "the future" is a series of images in the first dimension of time, based on memory-impressions, and inspired by desires for affirmation.

The relative reality of what we cannot but regard as the future is a present whose reflection may occasionally be perceived in the form of a memory-impression of that present, which, although familiar to us in another dimension of time, we have not in fact experienced in the time-dimension along which our consciousness is travelling.

54 ∙– Work and Play - XI

Parables, Timing

"There is a tide . . ."

1. An inexperienced shot will fire at a partridge the moment he sees it. When this error is brought home to him he tends to go to the other extreme and to wait until the bird is out of range before he shoots.

An experienced shot, on the other hand, understands the curve of opportunity, aims with unhurried deliberation, and shoots at the summit of that curve. And, if for any reason, for instance the intervention of circumstances beyond his control, he misses the effective period of that curve of opportunity, he forbears to fire when he could only hope to wound the poor bird, and allows the occasion to pass as though it had never arisen.

2. If you prepare a feast for a friend and he does not respond to the invitation the cakes become stale and the ripe fruit has to be thrown away. If later on he decides to partake of the feast you had spread for him he will find the board bare or will have to be satisfied with whatever happens to be in the house.

3. Some people, instead of catching omnibuses when they stop, seem to make a point of missing them and then running after them in despair. Usually they have to walk home.

55 ·~ *Reality and Manifestation - XV*

"Freewill"—The Basis of an Apparent Illusion

The alternatives that appear to be offered us at every moment of our lives may not be the pure illusion that we have assumed them to be. It may be possible, theoretically at least, to "choose." But in practice it is unlikely that we often can, or that most of us ever do, for in order to "choose," that is to change the "alternative" that lies in front of us on the tramline of our one-dimensional displacement in time, we must necessarily have effected or undergone a change in ourselves—and that happens rarely, if ever, to many of us. But, admitting such a change, or the culminating moment of a process leading up to such a change, it would seem probable that we find the points ahead of us re-set and our tram switches over to a line that, at that moment, is running parallel to our own. On such an occasion we are unaware of any variation in our surroundings (or *are* we always unaware?), but we have in fact switched over into a parallel life.

But who are the "we" that have switched over? Who are the "we" that have experienced a change in our selves?

Satori should be the supreme example of such a changeover, and it is likely that all authentic "spiritual" experiences are so also, but there seems no reason to suppose that such a change is necessarily accompanied by any recognisable "experience" as such.

The change in the self that precipitates such an event should inevitably be a reduction of the fog of illusion that surrounds the relative self in the form of the supposed personality or fictitious ego, such reduction liberating the element of reality and enabling it to become conscious of life on a more brightly-lit plane.

But what becomes of the other trams which were left behind on the other line; won't they miss ours? And won't they be surprised to see ours on the new line to which we have switched over?

We are only using a metaphor, we are not describing something that exists as such. How difficult it is to bear that in mind! Let us say, then, that the "points" are a railway junction and that we change trains. Both trains run from a beginningless beginning and go on to an endless end, but one is on the Inner Circle and the other is on the Outer.

And let us remember: there are no trains anyhow, and no passengers, but only fluctuating force-fields in which energy pullulates in diverse patterns, energy that is conscious of itself.

Why should we suppose anything so "improbable" as parallel lives? Draw a diagram, or envisage one; for simplification consider two dimensions only—those of the surface of this sheet of paper. Our life follows, let us say, the dimension of these lines I am writing, from "left" to "right." The other dimension, in which I have just written and am about to write, we pass through; it stays put, it is eternity; in it are "past" and "future." But we cannot be "length" without "breadth"; we have to exist in the second dimension also (as in the third).

Therefore parallel lives are not a theory: they are demonstrable and inevitable. But the word "parallel" should perhaps be in inverted commas. Are there any words that should not?

56 · ~ Time and Space - XII

Reincarnation and Recurrence, 4

The most experienced and authentic of Western Buddhists, Alexandra David-Neel, had the courage to state that Buddhists who accept the doctrine of the inexistence of the ego could not at the same time believe in the popular notion of reincarnation.* Since the former is the core of the Buddha's teaching, and the latter universal in the East, it appears to be a case of "should" not rather than "could" not, and only among the elite a case of "do" not.

Physics, having arrived via the laboratory, the microscope, higher mathematics, and two thousand five hundred years of reasoning by means of a comparison of the opposites, at the conclusions enunciated by the Buddha, it would seem to be desirable to establish the sense in which the concept underlying the popular notion of reincarnation can be, or must be, a fact.

It has been pointed out that recurrence is the relatively easily understood form of that fact, that the concept of parallel

---

* *Ed. Note:* "La majorité des Bouddhistes qui ne comprennent pas la doctrine touchant l'inexistence d'un ego ont repris l'ancienne idée hindoue de la reincarnation d'un esprit toujours le même." (Article by Madame A. David Neel in "Essais sur le Bouddhisme en général et sur le Zen en partculier"—Robert Linssen, T. II, p. 157)

lives represents a step nearer to an accurate understanding, but may we not add that the "fact" itself is simply that there is no need either for *re*incarnation or for *re*currence—for neither incarnation nor occurrence ever ceases nor ever could cease.

᭢

Good Heavens! Can't we take the trouble to read the *Bhagavad Gita?*

"There never was a time when I did not exist, nor you, nor any of these kings. Nor is there any future in which we shall cease to be." (B.G. II. 12.)

57 · Work and Play - XII

Men and Women, 2

Do we not all wonder about the mystery of the relations between men and women? They have an urgent need of one another, and yet they rarely, if ever, understand one another. Usually a state of latent enmity exists between them, and unceasing conflict.

On analysis this conflict will be found to be a struggle for domination. And that supplies the key to what is really a very simple problem indeed.

The obstacle that lies between them is a fictitious ego, two fictitious egos. Only if they could *give themselves* could they ever really approach one another. But that constitutes sacrifice, sacrifice of the self, the only sacrifice there is.

Is it easy? Does it often happen? How many achieve it?

Has anyone ever seen it? Has it ever been done?

Men and Women, 3 (Loyalty and Confidence)

When men and women accuse one another of disloyalty it is almost invariably a question of fact with which they are concerned. The "facts," however, are of subsidiary importance, if indeed they have any. On examination they are found to be false, exaggerated, and nearly always misinterpreted.

In any event, and whatever they may be, if anything, they had to be. It should suffice to understand; instead of to misunderstand suppositions.

What is important, and the only thing, is the "fact" that one was able to suspect the other of "disloyalty," i.e. that he, or she, projected that evaluation from him or herself on to the other. For "loyalty" is not a thing-in-itself: it is integral in love. If the latter is present the former is present, and "disloyalty" is as unthinkable as breathing without air.

As long as illusory evaluations are projected, spontaneity is shut out, and it is only in spontaneity, which is living in the present, that any relationship really exists.

58 ·~ *Reality and Manifestation - XVI*

Personality

When an alliance of "me"s places the Sum of its energies at the disposal of its strongest member the result is what is known as a "powerful personality."

When the desires of such a combine coincide with what must be, the result is what is called a "successful man" (or woman); when such desires are in conflict with what must be, the result is described as an "unsuccessful" man—as opposed to a "failure," who is a "nobody," i.e. lacking in personality.

What is seen as "strong will" is merely such a concentration of desires flowing with, or against, the current of inevitability.

Integration

If we cut up a photograph or a picture into a dozen pieces and lay them, separated, on the floor we observe just that—a series of disconnected scraps of paper. But if we look at them through a minifying-glass we will find that we are looking at an integrated picture. Even a collection of disparate objects so regarded will assume a coherent form of some kind.

If we are ever able to refocus our vision so that we cut out the time-illusion, and obtain an instantaneous glimpse of the intemporal universe, all the objects around us, including ourselves which form part of them, will be revealed in their reality, that is reintegrated. And behind the fragments of our "me"s we shall recognise an "I"—for all will be consciousness or I-Reality.

"Thirty Blows"

How difficult it is to realise that it is our own fault! How difficult to give up blaming the other person!

The first thing to do—and that is easy—is to see that it could not be his fault, or hers. We don't blame leopards either for their spots or for their rough habits when they meet us in the jungle and dislike the look of us (when they live with us and lick our faces we think they are charming).

But if we realise that we are leopards too, or robots

activated by electronic impulses that follow a schema pre-set and dependent on habit-memory (or karma), how are we blameworthy either?

Merely because we think we know that we ought to know better. Merely because, or in so far as, we know that if we understood—not just intellectually, but in full living realisation—we should be free, awake, living in the present, responding adequately to all circumstances, and incapable of doing a stupid thing.

"Thirty blows," that is what we deserve; perhaps—who knows—all that we need.

59 ·~ Time and Space - XIII

Perception

"Seize the present"—what nonsense we talk! "We" know no such thing as a "present": everything we know is in the "past."

Light has taken *time* to traverse space between every object we see and our eyes that see it. Sound and olfactory waves have taken time to traverse space between their sources and our ears and noses. Even touch and taste are not instantaneous. How, then, could we seize anything in the present when all things sensorially perceived are already in the past when we perceive them?

Clearly the present cannot be apprehended via our sense-perceptions. Never by looking or listening, feeling, smelling, or tasting can we hope to make contact with the present.

We must seek a more direct method. Did I say "more direct"? So direct that the *event* and *ourselves* are one and the same *experience*. For there *is* identity between the "I" and the

"Now."

Etre Présent au Présent is to realise that identity.

Time, Movement, and Reality

The notion of freedom to choose what we shall do is a function of duality. If we transcend duality by a flash of intuition the illusion of choice automatically vanishes.

What is called karma in the East, and more recently in the West, that is the network, or spider's web, of so-called cause-and-effect, which orders our every gesture and renders us purely mechanical beings on the psycho-somatic plane, is also a function of duality and has no existence in reality. It, also, is laboratory apparatus.

It can be seen as a function of time, and the relations of time, movement, and duality are accurately represented in the armorial bearings of the Isle of Man.

"All our historical civilisations have been based on the reality of the 'me' as a being, and, as a result, have been sub-human." (Carlo Suarès: *La Comédie Psychologiquè,* p. 66.)

Just so.

60 ·- Vale

Finita la Commedia

Our whole life is a comedy. We know that time is only a defect of vision, not essentially different from wearing an optical instrument through which everything might be represented inverted or in small pieces, yet everything we do, and nearly everything we say and think, is based on our acceptance of time as a reality.

We know that, on the plane on which we live our daily lives, we do what we must, and cannot do otherwise, yet we not only praise and blame ourselves and others, but we implicitly and explicitly accept the whole social and political structure which is based on the absurdity that everybody is free to do as he will and is responsible for each of his actions.

But supposing we were to real-ise and *live* what we know intellectually, in every hour and detail of our lives?

No, I am not going to explain what would happen. People are not required to think for one another. The facts have been demonstrated: it is for us to apply them to our minds and to our lives. It is for us to live them. And to take the consequences.

For we are free to real-ise, and this may be the only freedom we have. The fact of so doing should effect a change in our selves and enable us to *live* what has become real to us.

Each of us is free to—
    Recognise that he is a Dividual,
    Know that his only reality is an Unself,
    Realise the state of an Imperson.

Colophon

One day some learned men were discussing the composition of the moon. A small boy, who was listening, glanced up at the sky and announced, "It's only a sixpence," and laughed.

Many years later the small boy, become a man, looked at the moon through a telescope. What he saw interested him so much that he spent the following years studying it. But the longer he studied the more puzzled he became, until he despaired of ever understanding the composition of the moon, its origin, function, and destiny. Then one day the multifarious data began to fall into place, and the time came when he knew all that there was to be known about the moon. When questioned by the curious he was able to answer, "The moon? It is simple . . ." and he gave them a clear definition of what constituted the moon in a few dozen scientific terms.

After some years a small boy, hearing of his fame as an astronomer, said to him, "The moon is just a sixpence, isn't it? My nanny says it's a pearl, but I don't believe her." The man thought for a moment and replied, "Young man, you may well be right, though your nanny's theory may be right also." "But I thought you knew all about the moon?" the little boy said in surprise. "Once upon a time I thought I did," the man answered, "but now I know that I know nothing. You see, I collected all the facts that could be obtained, and then one day I realised that the facts themselves were unreal things, products of the human imagination." "So what have you decided to do about it?" asked the little boy.

"I am building a rocket so that I can go and see for myself," replied the learned man. "Will you come with me?"

The boy thought for a moment and laughed. "No thanks," he decided, "don't think I'll come." "Why not?" "I can see that the moon is a sixpence without going up in the air to bring it back."

Index

See also Table of Contents.
Titles of sections are in italics.
References are to the numbered sections, not to page numbers.

Action and Non-Action, 1, 2 and 3; **1, 13,** 18, **37;**
actions, 1, 5, 14, 18, 33, 38, 43, 45
"All the World's a Stage, and All the Men and Women Merely Players," 38
Ananda, see *Bliss*
Appearance as Reflection of Reality, **18**
Applied Zen and Real Zen, **23**
Aspects of Not-Being, 1 and 2; **1, 13**
Atman, 33, 36
attachment, 10, 14, 25, 29
non-attachment, 10, 16, 23, 24, 25, 29
attainment, 5, 15, 18, 23
authorship, *vii,* 23

be, 1, 13, 14, 56
Being—Not-Being, 1, 13, 18, 22, 34, 45
Benoit, Hubert, *v,* 13
Between Ourselves, **22**
Bhagavad Gita, 14, 56
birth, 2, 3, 11, 15, 18, 26, 34, 53
Bliss, **41**
Bodhidharma, 10, 16, 22
bodhisattva, 24
Body, **31**
Broglie, Louis de, 51
Buddha, 2, 56, 12, 14, 17, 21, 18, 22, 23, 36, 47, 29, 30, 39, 40
Buddha Nature, 1, 28, **33**
buddhi, 30, 33, 40, 42
Buddhism, 10, 12, 14, 18, 40

Canute, 50
Caritas, 16, 24, 40, 41, 42, 43, 50
Cassandra, **51**
cats, 3, 40
Cause and Effect: The Result of What Hasn't Happened, **51**
cause and effect, 13, 17, 19, 33, 39, 50, 51, 56
Chang Chan, 19
change (ourselves), 50, 51, 53
Choice, 18, **48,** 55, 59
Christians, 14
Chuang Tzu, 10, 12, 13, 18

civilisation, 50, 56
cognition, 11
Comment on the Essential Doctrine of the Lankovatara Sutra, **18**
concept, 18, 25, 27, 29, 30, 49
consciousness, 6, 7, 17, 18, 19, 25, 27
    organic, 9
contradictions, 30
correct action, see *Action and Non-Action*
Credo, **35**

David-Neel, 56
death, 2, 3, 11, 15, 17, 18, 26, 30, 34, 53
Debris, 1 and 2; **18, 19**
De-Bunking Time, **30**
Definition of Civilisation, **50**
desire, 2, 18, 33, 39, 41, 42, 43
Detachment, **29,** 39, 43
Dharma, 47
Dhyana, 10, 16, 23, 29
Dialogue, 1 and 2; **29**
Differentiation, **2**
dimensions
    Physics and Metaphysics, 10, 16, 23, 25, 27, 29, 49
    Reality and Manifestation, 13, 18, 24, 28, 30
    Time and Space, 2, 7, 11, 17, 19, 26, 53
    Work and Play, 50
Dimensions of the Mind, 1 and 2; **25, 27**
Dimensions of Space, **2**
direct cognition, 8, 15, 18, 29
Direct Perception, **11**

discipline, 10, 13, 15, 23, 28, 33, 39, 40
Disciplines, **33**
discourse, 18, 23, 47
Discrimination and Discrimination, **24**
do, doing, 1, 13, 29, 47, 50
dogma, 3, 10, 14, 51
Dreams, 11, **13,** 18
Dualism, **18**
    dualistic-duality, 10, 18, 59
Dufresne, 18, 30
duties, 5

ego, me, self, 1, 4, 10, 13, 15, 16, 18, 22, 24, 27, 28, 30, 33, 35, 39, 41, 45, 50, 52, 55, 57, 58
Einstein, 50
Ends as Means, **43**
energy, 18, 40
enlightenment, 10, 23, 24, 27, 36, 53
Eternal Present, **26**
Eternity, **34**
Eternity and Passing Time, **2**
Evolution of the Ego, **24**
existence, 1, 22
Eye That Cannot See Itself, **30, 40**

Father, The, **33**
Find Out Who It Is Who Is Predestined or Has Free-Will, **43**
Finita la Commedia, **60**
forgiveness, 30
Franklin, Benjamin, 40
freewill, 3, 16, 37, 43, 48, 53, 60

Freewill and Reality, **18**
Freewill - The Basis of an Apparent Illusion, **55**
From the Beginning Nothing Exists, **51**
Frontier, **40**
future, 2, 6, 14, 26, 28, 29, 53

Garrick, David, 38
Goose, and Its Apparent Bottle. It's Out! **29**
Government, **9**
Grace, 37, 47
Gurdjieff, 18

Hard Words, 1 and 2; **30**
Health, **9**
Heraclitus, 2
Hsi Yun, 23, 24, 28, 29, 30, 36, 39, 40
Huang Po, see Hsi Yun
Hui Hai, 16, 18, 23, 24, 28
Hui Neng, 10, 22, 24, 36, 40, 47, 51
humility, 1, 5, 13, 18, 43

I-Reality, 1, 10, 15, 28, 33, 36, 38, 39, 43, 49, 53, 59
identification, 23, 30, 38, 39, 43, 45, 49
Illusion of Continuous Individuality, **15**
Illusory Element of the Ego, **4**
immobility, 1, 2, 19, 32
inaction, see *Action and Non-Action*
instruction, 48
integrated man, 40, 43, 49
Integration, **58**

intellect, intellection, 10, 23, 24, 30, 36, 39
intellectual comprehension, 23, 36, 39, 43, 45
Intrinsic Value of Manifestation, **30**
intuition, 7, 11, 18, 59
intuitive cognition, 25, 27
intuitive comprehension, 23, 36, 39, 47

Jesus, 5, 9, 14, 23, 28, 39
Jivan Mukta, 18, 36, 40, 41, 42, 47
Judge Not, 5, **33**

Kant, 2, 11, 19
karma, 38, 58, 59
ken-sho, 23
Kingdom of Heaven Is Within, **11**
knowledge, 1, 8, 18, 23
Krishna, Sri, 14, 39
Krishnamurti, 40

Lao Tzu, *v,* 10, 12, 13, 18, 37
liberated man, 18, 41
liberation, 10, 13, 17, 21, 36, 45
life, 1, 2, 3, 6, 11, 26, 53, 55, 60
light, 2, 7, 11, 50, 57
Lin Chi, see Rinzai
Linssen, 41, 49, 53
Live Thought or Dead? The Zen Point of View, **23**
logic, 30
Logic and Superlogic, **30**
Long Fingers, **28**

Love, 1, 2 and 3; 16, **41**, 42, 43, **44**, **50**, 52
Love and Sex, **50**
Loyalty, 57

Maharshi, The, 28, 36, 37, 38, 39, 40, 43, 47, 48
Mad Monkeys, **13**, 1
Man is an Electronic Apparatus, **40**
manifestation, 30
matter, 3, 15, 51
Maya, 19, 22, 36, 39
meditation, 10, 16, 23
memory, 1, 2, 6, 10, 15, 17, 18, 21, 22, 29
  habit, 53, 58
  impressions, 53
Men and Women, 1 and 2; **20**, 57
Mind, 10, 13, 15, 18, 27, 29, 30, 40, 47
mind, 3, 6, 8, 11, 12, 18, 28, 29, 30, 46, 47
Mind Is Not Mind, **30**
Motion, **2**, 18, 19
movement, 2, 7
Movement Is Within, **11**
Myth of Forgiveness, **30**

Nationalism, **50**
Neither Subjective nor Objective, **13**
Nietzsche, 50
No Merit Whatsoever, **16**
Normal and Abnormal, **29**
noumena, 2, 6, 7

Only Truth, **18**

opposites, 1, 10, 16, 18, 40, 49, 56
Ouspensky, 2, 3, **13**, 23

Parables, Timing, **54**
Parallelism of Lives, **53**
Paravritti, 22, 23, 47
past, 2, 6, 11, 17, 26, 53, 59
Past and Future, 1 and 2; **2**, **53**
P'ei Hsin, 30
Perception, 11, 49, **59**
perceptions, 2, 8, 16, 18, 22
percepts, 18, 25, 27, 29, 49
Percepts, Concepts and Direct Cognition, **29**
Personality, **58**
phenomena, 2, 6, 7, 16, 17, 24, 30
Phenomenal Self and the Illusory Self, **13**
plane of being, 1, 5, 13, 23, 41
plane of existing, 1, 5, 6, 23, 40, 41; see Plane of Being
Pope, the, 47
possession, 20, 42, 50
  possessiveness, 41
Prajna, 8, 18, 29
Preparation for Satori, **47**
Presence in the Present, **49**
Present, **32**
Primaires, **46**
Progress? **43**
Promises, **50**
Prophecy, **26**
Prosperity, **5**
psychoanalyst, 19
Pythagoras, 53

Ramakrishna, 36

reaction, 1, 18
real vision, 18, 50,
realisation, 10, 15, 18, 23, 28, 39, 40, 41
Realisation by Non-Action, **39**
reality, 2, 11, 13, 19, 27, 29, 30, 39, 41, 47, 49, 50, 52, etc.
Reality and the Ego, 1, 2 and 3; **3, 13, 18**
Reality and Relativity, **13**
Reincarnation and Recurrence, 1, 2, 3 and 4; **2**, 5, **17**, 26, 38, **51**, 53, **56**
Relationship between Reality and Manifestation, **18**
Revaluation of Values, 1, 2 and 3; **2, 50, 52**
Rights and Possessions, **20**
Rinzai, 40

Sacrifice: A Quatrain, **50**
Sage, 15, 27
Saint, 15
St. Exupery, 5
St. Francis, 5
Sankalpas, 39
Satori, 1, 2, 3 and 4; 1, 6, **8, 10**, 11, **16**, 18, 23, 27, 38, 47, **49**, 50, 53, 55
Satori—Does It Exist? **23**
Scale of Observation Creates the Phenomenon, **17**
Schrodllger, 51
Screen of Time, **7**
Self Is Not Self, **43**
self-sacrifice, 42, 43, 57
sensorial perception, 2, 3, 11, 17, 18, 24
service, 5, 9, 14, 50, 52

Sex, **49**, 50
Shakespeare, 38, 51, 54
Shape of Life, **53**
Shen Hsiu, 47
Silence, 1, 2 and 3; 37, **47, 48**
spirit, 3, 50
spontaneity, 57
Stereoscopic Thinking, **49**
Suares, Carlo, 59
Suddenness of Satori, **47**
suffering, 5, 15, 18, 23, 35, 41
Sutra, 2; Prajnaparamita, 1; Diamond, 13, 21, 22, 30, 53; Hui Hai, 16; Hui Neng, 10; Lankavatara, 10, 18, 23, 53
Swami Nityabodhananda, 28
Swami Siddheswarananda, 13, 40, 49
Symbols, **11**

Talleyrand, 23
Tao, Taoist, Taoism, 10, 12, 18, 19, 24, 40
Tao Te Ching, 12
Tathagata Declares That Characteristics Are Not Characteristics, **13**
Thirty Blows, **58**
T-Bomb, **26**
Time, Movement and Reality, **59**
Transcending the Self—Which? **15**
truth, 3, 13, 18

Union, **42**
Upadesa, 47, 48

values, 2, 10, 18, 50

Vedanta, 36
Vida Es Sueño, **11**
Vijnana, 8
Vivekananda, 36, 40
void, 12, 13, 24, 27, 30, 41
Void: What Is It? **24**

Wake Up! **45**
Walking through the Mirage, **15**
Wasps, **23**
Wei Lang, see Hui Neng
*What Did the Monk Realise
   When Overtaken by a So-
   called Satori Experience?* **6**
What Is Zen? 1, 2, and 3; **10,
   12, 16**
will, 18, 39, 49, 50, 58
within, 11, 18, 23, 27, 28, 29,
   32
Words, Words, **5**
work, 13, 14
Work as Service, **14**

zeal, 23
Zen:
   characteristics, 10, 3, 15, 23,
      48, 50
   history, 10, 12, 18, 40
   "I", 15, 28
   method, 10, 8, 23, 24, 29,
      41, 53
   mondo and koans, 30, 47,
      48
   No-Mind, 10, 16
   object, 10
   Satori, 8, 47, 49
   technique, 10, 16, 18, 23, 41

Sentient Publications, LLC publishes books on cultural creativity, experimental education, transformative spirituality, holistic health, new science, and ecology, approached from an integral viewpoint. Our authors are intensely interested in exploring the nature of life from fresh perspectives, addressing life's great questions, and fostering the full expression of the human potential. Sentient Publication's books arise from the spirit of inquiry and the richness of the inherent dialogue between writer and reader.

We are very interested in hearing from our readers. To direct suggestions or comments to us, or to be added to our mailing list, please contact:

SENTIENT PUBLICATIONS, LLC
1113 Spruce Street
Boulder, CO 80302
303.443.2188
contact@sentientpublications.com
www.sentientpublications.com

Printed in Great Britain
by Amazon

24760533R00101